The

Dreammaker's

Apprentice

Other books by Arnold Mindell

Quantum Mind: The Edge Between Physics and Psychology

Sitting in the Fire: Large Group Transformation Using
  Conflict and Diversity

The Shaman's Body: A New Shamanism for Transforming
  Health, Relationships, and Community

The Leader as Martial Artist: An Introduction to Deep
  Democracy

The Year I: Global Process Work with Planetary Tensions

Inner Dreambodywork: Working on Yourself Alone

Riding the Horse Backwards: Process Work in Theory
  and Practice

Coma, Key to Awakening: Working with the Dreambody
  near Death

City Shadows: Psychological Interventions in Psychiatry

The Dreambody in Relationships

River's Way: The Process Science of the Dreambody

Working with the Dreaming Body

Dreambody: The Body's Role in Revealing the Self

Dreaming While Awake: Techniques for 24-Hour
  Lucid Dreaming

ARNOLD MINDELL, PH.D.

The

Dreammaker's

Apprentice

Using Heightened States of Consciousness to Interpret Dreams

HAMPTON ROADS
PUBLISHING COMPANY, INC.

Cover design by Marjoram Productions
Cover photo by PictureQuest
Interior art by Rebecca Parrish

Hampton Roads Publishing Company, Inc.
1125 Stoney Ridge Road
Charlottesville, VA 22902

434-296-2772
fax: 434-296-5096
e-mail: hrpc@hrpub.com
www.hrpub.com

If you are unable to order this book from your local bookseller, you may
order directly from the publisher. Call 1-800-766-8009, toll-free.

Library of Congress Catalog Card Number: 2001094964

ISBN 1-57174-229-8

10 9 8 7 6 5 4 3 2 1

Printed on acid-free paper in Canada

Contents

List of Illustrations:
Diagrams and Pictures

Preface

In *The Dreammaker's Apprentice*, I draw together ideas I have developed about dreamwork over the past thirty-six years of practice. This book updates the Jungian, Gestalt, and process-oriented dreamwork techniques I am familiar with or have developed. The basic idea of the present book is that dreams can be understood by watching carefully how we use our attention, how we move, and what we experience in our bodies and in our altered states of consciousness.

The new methods described in this book come from my research on the connections between psychology and physics. (See *The Quantum Mind* and *Dreaming While Awake: Techniques for 24-Hour Lucid Dreaming.*) My last book, *Dreaming While Awake,* is about "the Dreaming"; that is, about the subtle, sentient experiences from which all our dreams and experiences emerge. I show in *Dreaming While Awake* how the Dreaming's subtle sensations precede even fantasy. Feeling these sensations leads to new ways of working with body and relationship problems. Now in the present book, I show how experience of these most subtle sensations leads to new dreamwork theories and methods.

I thank my teacher in dreamwork, C. G. Jung, for his daring ability to see into the meaning of dreams. I have never met him in person, but see him regularly in my dreams. Thanks to Barbara Hannah, who taught me how to see dreams happening in the moment. She told me to seek out the help of Marie Louise von Franz, one of Jung's main students, to interpret the dream itself. Marie Louise was a mastermind at dreamwork. Dr. Franz Riklin helped me understand the living meaning of dreams.

These teachers and many others from the Jungian community synthesized Jung's ideas and showed me how to practice them. Many of their ideas, as well as many of Jung's, have never come out in print. I may have unconsciously merged or incorporated his and their ideas with my own concepts presented in this book. I want to thank all of these teachers for their teachings and influence on me.

My Background

I first studied dreamwork in Zurich, Switzerland, where I completed my studies in Jungian psychology in 1969 at the C. G. Jung Institute. After opening my practice on the Lake of Zurich, I eventually became a Jungian training analyst.

After my Jungian studies, I completed a doctorate in psychology at the Union Institute in Cincinnati, Ohio. During our free time after classes in the evenings at the Institute, a group of teachers and fellow students began coming to my room to ask me about dreams, since I was the only one who knew much about dreams. There was a radical and enthusiastic atmosphere among those students and teachers during the early 1970s; we felt the freedom to explore anything. In the midst of intense, all-night discussions, I made a discovery that was crucial to my own development.

I found, to my own surprise, that to be a good dream interpreter, you did not have to go through the same rigorous training program in dreams and myths as I had been through to understand dreams. I noticed that dreams become understandable with the help of an empirical attitude; that is, by paying strict attention to what the dreamer experienced and how she moved and spoke. I found myself saying repeatedly, "Notice what the dreaming process is doing in the moment in the body, how the dreamer is sitting, what she says, and what her feelings are. Watch her body and you will understand her dreams!"

What a discovery! Dreams happen not only at night. Even when someone is not telling a dream, you can see the dream trying to happen right in front of you during the daytime! The body itself is dreaming! I was so thrilled with this idea, I wrote *Dreambody,* which was published in 1980.

For example, a dreamer told me she dreamed that the Moon transformed into an eye through which she could see. Intellectually, I thought the dream meant she should see through the eyes of the lunar world, of the dream world. The dreamer liked my dream interpretation but could not really feel what I was talking about. Moreover, I did not really know what I was talking about! What does "seeing through the eye of the Moon or dreams" *really* mean?

In any case, I noticed the dreamer yawning and asked her what that yawning was like for her. She replied, "It makes me sleepy and I feel like resting." Therefore, I followed those impulses to rest and suggested to her, "Let yourself rest." As she let herself rest, she said, "I feel dreamy . . . aha! Now I know what that means, to see through the eye of the Moon." She understood her dream because she experienced how that dreamy state turned into a "dreamy" way of looking at the world. Her body was "dreaming"; it was in a "nighttime," "moonlight" state, so to speak.

Everyone in my first dream group thought my new approach was great—except someone sitting in the corner who had so much hair over her face that she could barely see what the dreamer who was telling the dream was doing. When I asked her what she was doing to interpret dreams so well, even though she was not carefully observing the dreamer, she simply said, she followed her *own* experience as well as the dreamer's. Although she came with the others to my dream group every evening during my studies, I never learned her name, so I cannot thank her sufficiently today. She added to what I had already learned: to understand someone else's dreams, follow your own and/or the other person's experience!

After I got my Ph.D., my Zurich-Jungian dreamwork practice became "dreambodywork" as I incorporated my own empirical method connecting the experience of body symptoms with the nighttime dreams. Two books came out of this focus: *Dreambody,* which primarily explores the body experience behind symbols, and *Working with the Dreaming Body,* which is mainly about using perceptual channels and process thinking in body and dreamwork.

By the 1980s, I felt constrained by dreambodywork and began to notice how spontaneous movements (such as tremors and twitches) and body signals (such as hand gestures and vocal tones) people make during relationship and group interactions can also be seen in the dreams. In other words, dreams not only are reflected in body symptoms, but also can be seen in unintentional body signals. This led me to write my *Dreambody in Relationships*.

I was thrilled to incorporate the teachings of Buddhist meditation teachers, Carlos Castaneda's shaman Don Juan Matus, and mystics such as Howard Thurman into my work, which today I call process work, or process-oriented psychology. This work has a broad spectrum of application whose outer limits we are still exploring today.

Thus the present book on dreams comes from an extensive practice connecting the dreams of individuals to body, relationship, and group experiences. Working with people of various nationalities, sexual orientations, races, and religions, in every imaginable state of health, has helped to broaden my perception of what constitutes the "normal" from my originally less inclusive white, heterosexual, middle class, American male education.

Acknowledgments

Besides the teachers, friends, and clients already mentioned, many others have contributed to what I know about dreams and dreamwork. Thank you, dear thousands of dreamers, for helping me learn dreamwork.

I want to thank Michael Murphy and the Esalen Institute in California for having invited Amy and me in 1987 to be the "in-house teachers" there. My background and interest in the Gestalt therapy practiced at Esalen have been a great help to me in understanding dreams.

I am indebted to the Geriami shamans and their tribal community in Kenya for making dreams come alive for me. I am grateful to Aboriginal Australians and their healers who have worked with me for the experiences they gave me of Dreamtime. Native American groups such as the Haida Nation on the Queen Charlotte Island in Canada helped me explore and understand the Great Spirit in dreaming.

I have learned a great deal about dreaming from Zen Master Keido Fukushima of Kyoto and from the writings of other Buddhist teachers. Great support for the early phases of my work came from Swami Muktananda. I am also indebted to the teachings of Sri Ramana Maharshi. Without these teachers, I would have felt alone in my explorations of nondualistic experiences behind dreams.

I am indebted to the insights and editorial help of Margaret Ryan, and the final polishing work of Mary McAuley and Heike Spoddeck. Many constructive suggestions came from Julie Diamond, Reini Hauser, John Johnson, George Mecouch, Dawn Menken, and Carl Mindell. Richard Leviton at Hampton Roads has been a true inspiration in completing the present form of this work.

It is a great pleasure to thank my partner in all things, Amy Mindell. Amy worked through every paragraph of this book, and taught courses on dreamwork with me in various parts of the world. Whatever I could say about her would not be enough to convey the importance she has for me in general, and for the synthesis of ideas into written form in particular. We have long worked with one another on dreams, and experimented together and with hundreds of others on the material brought forward in this book.

1

WORKING ALONE ON DREAMS

How to Interpret Dreams by Dreaming

1

The Mystery and Meaning of Dreams

I want to know God's thoughts, the rest is details.
—Albert Einstein

When I was a child, my parents took me to the seashore, where I loved watching ocean waves crashing on the beach. When I asked what makes those waves so big, no one knew. At the age of five, I thought the movement of the waves must be due to the wind. However, on the day I asked that question, there was no wind. My father explained to me that ocean waves are not caused primarily by the wind, but rather by the Moon's gravitational pull on our Earth. What a thought! As the Moon goes around the Earth, it "tugs" on the water, so to speak, and makes waves—even when there is no wind!

This story about the Moon's invisible pull on the Earth came back to me when I began to wonder where dreams came from.

Like ocean waves, dreams seem to be due to the momentary problems of everyday reality (the wind) and the one-sided behavior of our everyday thinking. However, dreams do not come only from our one-sided behavior but are also influenced by the "pull" of what some Aboriginal people call the "Great Spirit" or the Dreammaker,[1] or the Dreaming.[2] The Dreammaker is like the Moon, that heavenly body in outer space that influences every one of us, though we do not often realize it. Just as both the wind and the gravitational pull of the Moon affect the ocean's waves, I will show in this book how both everyday life and the Dreammaker's mind influence dreams.

I will bring forward exercises and experiments that give us access to that invisible Dreammaker's mind, and the "tug" we feel from subtle, usually forgotten, altered states of consciousness and mystical experiences that occur continuously throughout both day and night. This book is about learning to experience these altered states, and using them to understand the meaning of dreams. In this way we can each know, in our own way, the thoughts of God and the meaning of dreams—the Dreammaker.

Just as I asked when I was a child what was behind the waves in the ocean, and just as we all have wondered at one time or another what lies behind dreams, Albert Einstein wanted to know the God that was behind the whole universe. Einstein died in 1955, but if he were alive today, I can imagine him saying, "I want to know 'God's thoughts'; knowing the mind of God is more important than anything else, including the interpretation of a dream."

---

[1] C. G. Jung used the term "Dreammaker" in everyday conversation.
[2] I explore the meaning of the Aboriginal term "the Dreaming" in chapter 1 of my *Dreaming While Awake*.

According to my interpretation of the mathematics behind quantum physics,[3] everyday reality arises out of rapid, imaginary, virtual, or dreamlike interactions between the observer and the observed. These mutual, dreamlike interactions—I call them "flirts"—are needed to explain quantum mechanics and the way in which observation of the real world takes place. In other words, what we call "you" and "I" are partially two interacting presences in an invisible world. From the viewpoint of that world, we cannot be sure who is the observed and who is the observer. It is as if both are part of the Dreammaker's mind, the Mind of God, thinking about Itself.

What does this interpretation of physics mean for dreamwork? Until now, dreamwork theories have been largely independent of the theories of physics. Now we have the beginnings of a theory and practice that connect dreamwork and everyday physics. Dreams are descriptions of a virtual world which, like the quantum world, cannot be directly measured. However, the dreamworld can be experienced. Like the invisible world of the mathematics of quantum mechanics, dreams describe interactions between virtual entities that are everywhere at all times. We can say all this more briefly using the jargon of science: Dreams are nonlocal and nontemporal.

What do "nonlocal" and "nontemporal" mean? If I dream of a grizzly bear in a forest, as far as everyday reality is concerned, that bear and forest are both nonlocal and nontemporal. The bear and the forest are everywhere, at any time. In the early morning while I am asleep and dreaming about that bear, I am nonlocal and nontemporal. As I awaken, however, I become Arny Mindell in a certain place and time. My alarm clock tells me to wake up out of that nonlocality and go to work in my office at a certain place.

---

[3] I explain my interpretation of quantum physics in my book *Quantum Mind: The Edge Between Physics and Psychology.*

Later that day, my nighttime dream about the bear may suddenly become clear to me, especially if I notice how excited I get about something. When I notice that I feel like roaring like a bear, I suddenly understand. Aha! That bear is an aspect of me. What I mean by understanding a dream is that I sense its nonlocal nature suddenly becoming local. In that moment, I realize that the nonlocal dream bear is part of my everyday self.

Dream theory that connects psychology to quantum physics suggests that our dreams are nonlocal and nontemporal. When we understand them, the erstwhile dreamer observes dreams at a certain place and time in everyday life. Understanding dreams "realizes" them—for example, that bear becomes a "real" part of me.

Two Levels of Dreamwork

The challenge I have set for myself is to develop a dreamwork that explains dreams on at least two levels:

• First, dreamwork should help us experience where dreams come from; that is, the virtual reality upon which everyday life is based, and the "thoughts of God."

• Second, dreamwork should help us understand a dream in terms of our everyday selves.

It is my belief that without the experience of the source of dreams, we cannot properly understand dreams. The aspect of dreamwork I stress in this book informs you about how to live your life better by living closer to that virtual source of dreams, the experience of the Dreaming and "thoughts of God." Also, when you live closer to the source of dreams, you sense and understand your everyday life as arising with all those things you call your problems and symptoms. When you know the Dreaming behind everyday life, problems no longer seem like frozen states, but are experienced as streams of creative power. You feel rooted in an awesome, unfathomable, but deeply enriching universe.

In an older dreamwork paradigm you might explain my bear dream by analyzing the symbol of the bear for me. You might say that a certain power is trying to enter my everyday life. That is an interpretation I can "integrate." Integration means discovering that something that is nonlocal can be found arising in a certain time and place; that is, within me.

In the newer dreamwork paradigm, you can also notice the bear's signals in my unintentional behavior, in the tendencies of my voice to growl like a bear even when I think I am acting quietly. In other words, you can hear or see the Dreaming or Einstein's "God's thoughts" popping up in my unintentional tendencies such as my bearlike signals. By pointing this out to me, you can suggest I take a moment and sense where those unintentional tendencies are coming from. By asking me such a question, you make me aware of deep experiences that seem to me like the source of my life. It is as if I can sense Dreammaker's thoughts.

Experiencing the mind of God helps me to understand the meaning of the bear dream in a new and profound manner. Experiencing the source of dreams and understanding their significance in everyday life are the goals of this book.

My Personal Story

Let me tell you a bit of my own story, about how I got interested in dreamwork. My first experience of psychotherapy was a remarkable session with Marie Louise von Franz, a Jungian analyst from Zurich, Switzerland. At that time I was twenty, an American student spending my junior year in Zurich. In my early weeks there, each night I was awakened by amazing dreams. One morning a student friend of mine told me to visit an "old witch," a Jungian analyst who lived on the Lake of Zurich. He said that she would know what to do with my dreams.

I nervously arrived at my first therapy session, which took place in an old apartment that seemed to be hanging over the lake. I wondered who this "witch" would be and was surprised to meet Dr. Marie Louise von Franz, who warmly greeted me at the door. She was not a witch at all, but a friendly, middle-aged, Austrian-Swiss woman, one of C. G. Jung's main successors.

I sat down and promptly told her my problem: I had been having too many amazing and weird dreams. She listened and then asked me to tell her one of my dreams. Not knowing anything about Jungian psychology, I shamelessly asked why she thought we should ponder dreams at all. Could we not find out what was wrong with me by just looking at my physical self? She patiently answered my bold question by saying that at present, the method she knew best was to ask about the dreams themselves. She explained that the "unconscious" could appear through dreams and tell me how to lead my life.

I persisted, insisting that dreams could not be the only way to understand myself. Why not speak directly to the "unconscious" itself? My studies in applied physics made the focus on dreams seem unnecessary. Could she not tell me about my problems by looking at my body, at the physical me, sitting in front of her? Her humble answer was that she did not know how to do that, and that the physicist's approach to the unconscious was something I should make a part of my research. She said someone named C. G. Jung would have been interested in such an approach but that he had died just a few weeks ago.

Indeed, on June 7, 1961, C. G. Jung had died. He had been fascinated by the relationship between dreams and physical reality. In fact, he had spent the last years of his life exploring the connections between psychology and physics with the Nobel prizewinning physicist Wolfgang Pauli. Just before he died, Jung asked von Franz to carry on his research. After I became less impertinent, she spoke with me in depth about his and her new ideas about numbers, synchronicity, psychology, and physics. Over time, our relationship developed multiple levels. She was my therapist, but I was also her friend and support in the work she was doing. (The concept of "dual relationships"—that is, of relationships involving multiple roles such as therapist, client, friend, research support, etc.—was not known at that time.) In any case, she finally wrote a book on the unitary background to psychology and physics called *Number and Time.*[4]

My development of process work, or process-oriented psychology as it is also called, grew out of those early conversations with von Franz. I answered my own question—Why look at dreams to understand the unconscious?—by doing the research that preceded the publication of my first book, *The Dreambody,* in 1982.[5] There I showed how dreams could be seen to manifest in the body.

Dreams, Dreaming, and Dreamwork

I have always been more interested in the way in which dreams appear in various aspects of everyday reality than in the dream images themselves. Today it is clear to me that dreams are just one of the manifestations of "the unconscious," which I will call, from now on, "the Dreaming." I love Jung's term, "the unconscious." Nevertheless, in my imagination, today he would prefer the term "the Dreaming" because of its connection with Aboriginal

---

[4]In 1974, Northwestern University Press first printed von Franz's formidable book, which speaks mainly about number theory.
[5]See *Dreambody,* recently republished by Lao Tse Press.

Australians and with cultures that support simultaneous awareness of dreaming and wakeful consciousness.

According to Aboriginal peoples, the Dreaming is the mysterious power, the invisible energy behind everything we look at. As I show in *Quantum Mind: The Edge Between Physics and Psychology,* experiences of Dreaming can be seen to be patterned in the so-called wave function, the basic mathematical pattern behind reality. Aboriginal Australians say the Dreaming is a subtle force that makes you gravitate toward things, that makes you look toward something, before you consciously observe it. According to Aboriginal Australians, the Dreaming is the power and pattern that create physical reality. They explain it succinctly: You can kill the kangaroo, but you cannot kill its essence, the "Kangaroo Dreaming."

The Dreaming behind your dreams, your body symptoms, your unconscious gestures and signals has been given many names by various peoples throughout history. While a physicist might think of the Dreaming in terms of the wave function, the mathematical realm behind physical reality, Jews, Christians, or Muslims might refer to It as Yahweh, God, or Allah. Hindus or Buddhists might call It Brahman, the Void, or Buddha Mind.

Dreaming is not just a spiritual or mystical factor; it is empirical, an experience, something everyone senses. For example, if you train your awareness, you can sense that you do not simply move, but that your every move is preceded by a "tendency" to move in a certain direction. In short, the Dreaming is the *tendency* you feel for moving and thinking; it is the tendency that you sense to feel, see, or hear just before you actually feel, see, or hear something.

Experiment with Dreaming

Take a moment, relax, and if you are comfortable with closing your eyes, close them in order to complete this little experiment.

Notice the slightest subtle tendency inside your body to move. After you sense this tendency, follow it, and let your body move in the direction of that tendency. For example, if you have a tendency to relax your neck and let your head fall, then let it fall, and follow that tendency. If you feel that your arms have a tendency to stretch, then follow that tendency, let it "unfold," that is, express itself.

Notice how and where you move, and notice the fantasies connected with the movements you make. For example, if you find a tendency to stand, then stand up, and notice what you experience and fantasize about standing up, or "taking a stand."

My point is that the tendency to move in one direction or another is due to the force of the Dreaming. When you notice the Dreaming and Its tendencies, you are noticing the origins of your dreams. In other words, the Dreaming tendencies you experience preceding your movements (also preceding your words and everything else you do and think, including your dreams) can be found directly or indirectly in the patterns of your dreams. Dreaming underlies the dreams and your tendencies to move. Dreaming is basic to life itself.

Remember the woman I mentioned in the Preface, who dreamed that the Moon became an eye through which she could see? Recall that she understood her dream by noticing the tendency of her body to yawn and relax. In other words, the Dreaming, the tendencies and impulses to relax, were bringing her into a night-time or "lunar" world from which she could observe reality. She then experienced the meaning of her dream in which the Moon became an eye through which she could see. The meaning of the dream for her was to see through relaxed, dreamlike, foggy states of consciousness, through the eye of the Moon.

In their earliest stages, tendencies to yawn and relax simply happen; she experienced them simply as tiredness. However, when such subtle tendencies are not appreciated, they seem to amplify themselves and can become body symptoms.

The way in which tendencies self-amplify seems to follow the general description (in physics) of quantum phenomena, which amplify and reflect themselves to become real, and (in Aboriginal traditions and personal experience) of the Dreaming phenomenon, which tends to manifest in reality. For example, several weeks after her dream of the Moon, the dreamer suddenly fainted, falling to the floor, giving herself a slight concussion. Seeing through the eyes of the Moon was a symbolic statement of a tendency that had been trying to evolve for some time and finally manifested as fainting.

The point is that awareness of tendencies allows you to experience the thoughts of God, the Dreammaker's power of Dreaming, and the intelligence behind dreams and symptoms. In my experience, it seems that awareness of these tendencies may also help to relieve some symptoms.

Brief History of Dreamwork

My work with dreams stems from my interest in physics as well as my background in psychology and the social sciences. Quantum mechanics first introduced me to the concept of "tendencies." In the 1920s, the brilliant German physicist, Werner Heisenberg, one of the founders of quantum mechanics, interpreted the enigmatic quantum wave function, the formula physicists use to understand reality.[6] Heisenberg suggested that the wave function (more precisely, the amplitude of the wave function) represented the tendency for something to happen in reality. According to Heisenberg,

---

[6]The quantum wave function, or "wave function," is a mathematical pattern that physicists can use to calculate the properties of particles.

the quantum wave function is a "tendency" that gives rise to every-day reality.[7]

The quantum theory of matter and the concept of the "subconscious" both appeared in the early 1900s. Albert Einstein, Sigmund Freud, and many others in the West began the twentieth century by rediscovering the unknown in terms of quantum mechanics and dreams. It seems as if, after centuries of trying to convert shamanistic cultures and "primitives" to modern times, by the turn of the twentieth century, European cultures were changing. Theoretical physics and depth psychology were returning to the unknown through the discoveries of quantum physics and the psychology of the unconscious.

In his seminal book in 1906, *The Varieties of Religious Experience,* William James said, "It is as if there were in the human consciousness a sense of reality, a feeling of objective presence, a perception of what we may call 'something there,' more deep and more general than any of the particular 'senses.'"[8] James was interested in the "living phenomena before it is split by the subject-object dichotomy." He said, "feelings are the germs and starting point, and thoughts the developed tree."[9]

Sigmund Freud published *The Interpretation of Dreams* in 1900. Freud will surely be remembered for his courage to investigate dreams, for his discovery of the "subconscious," the idea of repression, and the idea that the content of dreams is linked to the fact that certain experiences are deemed unacceptable to the conscious mind. Although many of Freud's theories on the function of dreams,

---

[7]To be more specific, the quantum wave function is the tendency that gives rise to the probabilistic nature of everyday reality. Mathematically speaking, "conjugating" this function for a certain event gives the probability that that event will occur. See my *Quantum Mind,* chapters 14 and 15, for more information about the meaning of this mathematics.

[8]See his important *The Varieties of Religious Experience,* page 55.

[9]This too comes from James's *The Varieties of Religious Experience,* page 218.

such as wish fulfillment, are no longer widely used, his idea that dreams were "the royal road to the unconscious" led the way for the dream to become the central focus of depth psychologists.

Jung saw that dreams had a "finalistic" quality, a purpose behind them. Jung talked about complexes and archetypes and the idea of compensation. He saw that many dream images and stories compensate for the limitations of our everyday mind. Jung pioneered the idea that there were practical aspects of dreams, which you could integrate into your daily life, while also respecting that unfathomable aspect of the "unconscious," which he likened to the world of quantum physics. He spoke often in his last major work, *Mysterium Coniunctionis,* of needing to find that one world, the world the alchemists called the "*Unus Mundus,*" from which both psychology and physics could spring. The Dreaming and the thoughts of God are descriptions of this unifying world.

In any case, there were many thinkers associated with the history and development of dreamwork. I think of the work of Alfred Adler, Erik Erickson, and Medard Boss. In the 1960s, at the Esalen Institute in Big Sur, California, Fritz Perls changed the face of dreamwork by making sure that each dream figure was experienced in what he called "the here and now." If you dreamed of a friend, Perls wanted you to be that friend, now.

More recently, pointing to this subtle, sentient background to reality, Professor Eugene Gendlin said in 1962 that a bodily sense underlies reality: "Experiencing is the constant, ever present, underlying phenomenon of inwardly sentient living, and therefore there is an experiential side of anything . . . within experiencing lies the mysteries of all that we are."[10]

Some of my friends and colleagues have updated the theory and applications of dreamwork. Jim Hillman's *The Dream and the*

---

[10]Gendlin said further, "Experiencing is pre-conceptual . . . it is a process, an activity, a functioning, not a bag of static things."

Underworld (1979) and his development of archetypal psychology focuses on respecting the experience of Dreaming, especially in the areas of myth-making. Pat Berry (1974 and 1978) has brought forward the idea that the dream is an end unto itself: "The dream's purpose is within the dream itself" and need not always be thought of "in reference to the dreamer's conscious attitude." Although the Dreaming is not seen as a living presence in the moment, Berry stresses that the dream's reason for being must not always be framed within the content of the dreamer's personal life.

Gayle Delaney (1996) helped popularize dreamwork by bringing it close to mainstream thinking. Stan Krippner (1988) deepened the application of dreamwork. Stephen LaBerge (1991) re-created interest in lucid dreaming through learning how to train dreamers to signal the onset of a dream while asleep. Patricia Garfield (1997) has been pioneering in relating dreamwork to the possibility of communication with the dead. More recently, Robbie Bosnak (1997) integrated Hillman's imaginal (realm of the soul) approach to dreams by suggesting the dreamer reenter the dream state while awake.

Hillman's classic *The Dream and the Underworld* warned that dreamwork should be "protective of those depths from which dreams rise . . . the imaginal, and all the hiding invisibilities that govern our lives." Hillman was reacting to the fact that, until then, dreamwork had focused on understanding dreams in terms of consensus reality, in terms of their significance for everyday life. Dreams were examined primarily for the meaning they had for the conscious mind, the "ego." Hillman pointed out that dreaming was important in and of itself.

The concept of meaningfulness is usually determined by the everyday mind. Yet, from the viewpoint of Dreaming, dreams are not primarily meaningful. They are images of unfolding powers, formless tendencies, and mysteries. Focusing on the meaningfulness dreams might have for the everyday mind favors your everyday

personality, but detours your attention from the mysterious experience of the unspeakable and ineffable Dreaming. In my experience,
this is something you can experience every moment of the day and
night. I shall not go further into the history of dreamwork at this
time, since others have done it already.[11]

Dreamwork and the Unknown

There have been many ways of approaching the deepest levels
of consciousness that gives rise to everyday reality (see figure 1).
While Jung and Freud studied dreams and made theories about the
unknown substratum of the human personality, calling it the "subconscious" or "unconscious," Aboriginal peoples and ancient
Chinese Taoists focused on the sentient, preverbalizable level, on
vague feelings and sensations. Aboriginal people called it
"Dreamtime;" the early alchemists called it the "*Unus Mundus*," the
One World. The Taoists spoke of the "Tao that can't be said."
Physicists speak of the unknown in terms of quantum mechanics,
where reality is imagined to arise through observation. The act of
observation is expressed mathematically in terms of the so-called
quantum wave function, a virtual field, which is composed of complex numbers. As I said earlier, quantum mechanics implies that the
essence of a material particle is spread all over space and time
before it is observed.

Native and Aboriginal ideas about dreams stress respect for the
power of Dreaming. Later I will show how Buddhist ideas help in
understanding the link between Dreaming and perception.

---

[11]See the good works of Pat Delaney, James Hall, and Montague Ullman in
the "Readings" section at the end of this book.

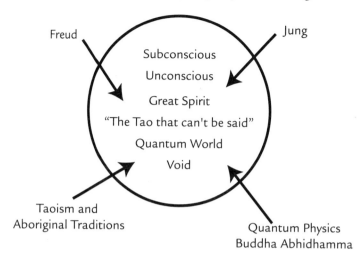

Figure 1. Different approaches to the unknown.

The Approach of This Book

As I have said, dreamwork has been focused mainly on relating the dream to the everyday mind. In this book, the focus will be on understanding dreams by noticing the Dreaming, the tendencies of the Dreammaker's mind that produce dreams. Most dreamworkers have typically believed that dreams manifest repressed material or contain archetypal patterns, or both. Dream therapists have generally focused on amplifying the content by making associations—exploring archetypal themes and role-playing dream figures. The conclusion of this type of dreamwork is usually a suggestion about what the dreamer needs to change, add to, or subtract from, in her everyday life.

In this book, I focus on training awareness to explore the tendencies and altered states of consciousness that give rise not only to dreams but to all your body experiences. Access to these altered states of the Dreaming enables you to understand your everyday self and your dreams from an entirely new perspective, from the viewpoint of the Dreammaker.

Emphasis is placed not on your gaining intellectual knowledge about dreams, but rather on your gaining a clearer sense of your relationship to infinity. While interpretative methods using previous knowledge can be very helpful, they relate you to the dream, not the Dreammaker; they relate you to the book, not the author, so to speak.

In short, from the viewpoint of Dreaming, dreams are pictures of ongoing creative experiences happening right now, every moment of the day in your body, feelings, and relationships.

In the earlier dreamwork methods, you were crucial, the center of each of your dreams. The dream and dreamer were crucial. In the new method, the Dreaming, not the dream or dreamer, is central (see figure 2).

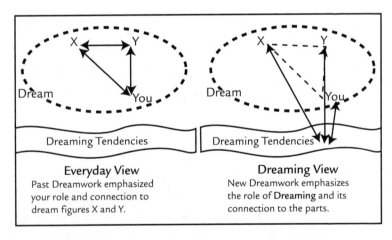

Figure 2. Everyday view and Dreaming view of dreams.

The Dreaming viewpoint is both psychological and spiritual. In the past, in the everyday view, you are central. In the Dreaming view, the Dreammaker's mind is central. In the older method, if you did not dream, something was missing. In the newer method, you are always dreaming and everyone is a dreamer. Both views are important and belong together.

Psychological and Spiritual Interpretation of Dreams

As I have indicated, there are two possible ways to understand dreams. They can be understood as parts of yourself you need to get to know better and also as manifestations of a presence, of the Dreammaker. The following experiment may help you to experience and clarify the differences between a psychological and a spiritual interpretation of dreams. A pencil and paper will help you to record and unfold your experiences.

1. Take a moment and recall a dream or part of a dream. For the purposes of this inner-work experiment, record only a short dream or a short fragment of a dream. If you like, write it down. Taking notes will make the experiment easier to do.

2. Now make any comments that come to mind about that dream fragment or one of its figures.

3. Put the dream fragment aside, and ask yourself if there is anything that has been bothering or fascinating you in the last day or two. Make a note of that as well. Also list any subjects, issues, people, or problems you usually try to avoid thinking about.

4. Now focus on your tendencies. Experiment with training your awareness and trusting your own experience. Take a moment, relax, even close your eyes, and sense your body. What are you

feeling, what feelings do you have that you have not yet noticed? What spontaneous movements would your body like to make that it has not yet made? What movements has your body not been allowed to do but yet still has a tendency to do? For example, does it want to relax? Does it want to get up and move? Sense your movement tendencies and let your body follow those tendencies. As you move, let your body "explain" its movements to you. If you are patient, your movement experience may explain itself.

This may take a few minutes. Be patient, especially if you are not used to following movement tendencies. Make a note about these motions and their possible significance for you.

5. Look at the answers and notes you took during the first four steps, especially at your Dreaming experiences in number four. See if they may in some way be connected to your dream fragment. If you think of the dream as a pictorialization of Dreaming tendencies trying to happen all day long, the movement tendencies that you experienced may give you an idea about the meaning of your dream. Note that meaning here.

Try to make the following two interpretations:

• Attempt an everyday interpretation of your dream. Tell yourself something about needing to expand your identity to include the figures or events in the dream.

• Make a spiritual interpretation of your dream using the idea that the Dreaming is a presence. Consider the tendencies as experiences that the Dreaming is trying to generate. Remember the sense of your movement tendencies and notice how the Dreaming is trying to unfold as a kind of presence in your life, in your movements, fantasies, interests, and so forth.

While the everyday interpretation of your dream focuses on the dream images, the spiritual interpretation is based on the experience of the energy that gives rise to those images. Seeing things from your viewpoint is probably more familiar to you than feeling experiences of the Dreaming, or according to Einstein, the thoughts of God. Your viewpoint and the experience of "Its" viewpoint are two very different worldviews. Your viewpoint is based on your problems, interests, and everyday life. "Its" viewpoint is based on a deep sense that is beyond your own personal life.

For example, in the situation I mentioned earlier in which a woman dreamed about seeing through the eyes of the Moon and later fainted, her Dreaming tendencies in the moment of the dreamwork with me were connected with yawning. While the everyday psychological interpretation might be that she is discovering how relaxing allows her to view things in new ways, the experience of the Dreaming tendency appearing in her yawning gives her a kind of spiritual interpretation, namely, the sense of "Its" presence in her life right now.

For the moment, it is important to consider that Dreaming manifests as tendencies and early signals or "presignals," and that you have to use your awareness of the subtlest perceptions to notice this Dreaming. Even though you may not yet have had much training in sensing subtle tendencies, you may have noticed in the previous exercise that if you pay attention to these subtle perceptions, your dreams seem less foreign.

Once you move closer to Dreaming, to your unformulated sensations, once you have trained your attention, the more you know what you will dream before you dream it. When you live close to the Dreaming, you notice that what happens in your fantasies, body feelings, and movements is not structured only by your ordinary thoughts. Something else is moving you, creating dreams, fantasies, and experiences. You may be able to sense the mind of God and, simultaneously, the meaning of dreams. Then you become the Dreammaker's apprentice.

The Thoughts of God and the Meaning of Dreams

The contents of this book are divided into four sections, each presenting a particular method of gaining access to altered states of consciousness that give you the ability to understand your dreams. In each of the four parts, the first chapter is theoretical. The last chapter of each section includes an extensive training exercise and method for doing dreamwork.

Part 1, "Working Alone on Dreams," focuses on how to work on dreams alone, by yourself. To do this, we will first examine the origin and the four dimensions of dreams and use a kind of breathwork to interpret your dreams. If you are interested in meditation, you will love this section.

Part 2, "Co-creative Dreaming," explores symbolic thinking and gives you a body sense of how dream images connect to body problems. Here I present a new form of dreamwork in which you and another person enter an altered state of consciousness together to unfold the meaning of dreams. Symbolic thinking is coupled with storytelling and shamanism. You will love this method if you are the least bit childlike or imaginative, or if you like mind-altering experiences.

Part 3, "Dreaming with Flirts," shows how dreams pictorialize tendencies and meditative experience. This method is especially suited to anyone interested in the Dreaming behind time and space. This section deals with learning to understand your dreams before you even have them.

Part 4, "Everyday Life as a Dream," focuses on working with people who say they don't dream. It shows how the Dreaming appears in "dreamdoors" such as special uses of language and music appearing in everyday consciousness and it shows how to go through those doors to separate realities.

 ## Things to Remember

1. The Mind of God or the Dreaming may be the source of your dreams and everyday reality.

2. To experience this source, you need to focus on the subtlest tendencies during your everyday life. Then you realize working on your dreams means getting to know the Dreammaker.

2

Interacting Realities

I recognize that Dreaming, like the quantum wave function, is at the edge of the known universe—it is weird, interesting, but challenging to explain in everyday terms. But then, learning to get along with such challenges is typical for individuals working at the forefront of human knowledge. "The truth of the matter is research is almost always without understanding," says University of Arizona physicist Johann Rafelski, whose specialty is the physics of the vacuum or empty space. "Physics doesn't require someone who's intelligent. It requires not taking for granted things which are happening around you."[12]

In one of his weekly "Mind Over Matter" columns in *The Los Angeles Times* ("Getting Comfortable With Confusion") K. C. Cole writes, "[G]o ahead. Dare to be stupid. But beware. Being stupid can be harder than you think. . . . By its very nature, the edge of knowledge is at the same time the edge of ignorance."

---

[12]I am thankful to Fred Kahne for pointing me to this *Los Angeles Times* June 6, 1999 article.

In quantum physics the invisible, immeasurable reality of what is called the quantum wave function gives rise to particles and, ultimately, to the infinity of forms that make up everyday reality. In other words, to understand the reality of matter, you have to give up what you thought was known and true, and accept that the quantum world may be inexplicable. Likewise, the invisible and immeasurable process of Dreaming gives rise to projections, dreams, and action in everyday reality.

A basic theme that is common to both physics and spiritual systems is the principle of an essence. In physics this essence may be the invisible quantum wavelike spaces which manifest as matter, while in spiritual traditions the essence may be one or more deities that inspire or manifest as events in everyday reality. I have been calling this essence "the Dreaming." If we think of the Dreaming as the inspiring force of some Dreammaker, Its plan might look like the picture below (see figure 3), which shows the Dreaming interacting with the reality of dreams and everyday consensus reality.

Figure 3. The Dreammaker's plan.

The arrow in the center of figure 3 indicates how everyday reality and its uncontrollable events arise out of the Dreaming. The dimensions of awareness relating to dreamwork that are indicated in the above plan may be summed up as follows:

1. Everyday life is consensual reality. In ordinary life, by common consent, we have an identity and exist at a certain time and in a specific location. We obey the laws of matter. We live our ordinary lives, focus on our friends, family, social situations, dreams, businesses, and world problems. We must identify ourselves as coming from a certain mixture of races, ethnic heritages, and religions; each of us is a certain age, has a certain health and strength. We are concerned with our bodies and material possessions and operate within the laws of physics. Until now, these laws imply and infer that nothing goes faster than the speed of light and that the invisible part of nature is less significant than what we can measure.

2. Dreams pattern consensual reality. Jung and others have shown that what we dream predicts the large patterns of our lives. If you dream about flying as a child, the chances are you choose a life based on spiritual things, and may have trouble dealing with everyday reality. Dreams occur during the night or daytime in events such as body symptoms or fantasies that at first may seem meaningless because their content appears to be fragmented or incomplete and unintentional. Dreams seem surprising, uncomfortable, or too incredible to focus on. Nevertheless, we often remember them. On close inspection, it turns out that these dreams pattern all of our unconscious, unintentional experiences in everyday life.

3. Dreaming is the origin of dreams. By training our attention, we can notice the Dreaming going on in the subtlest aspects of perception, whose essence cannot be easily seen or verbalized. We experience the Dreaming process as the tendency or inspiration to imagine and do things. We think we imagine something, but the inspiration

for imagining comes from the Dreaming that we have little control over. We think that we think or walk with our legs, but the impulse behind our thinking and walking is an experience that remains an incomprehensible mystery to the rational, waking mind. We are channels for the Dreammaker's impulses.

From our viewpoint, the viewpoint of our everyday selves or the "little me," the signals between the world and ourselves are due either to the world or to us. However, from the viewpoint of the Dreammaker's mind, it is not we who perceive, but rather perception happens to us. There is no distinguishable separation between observer and observed in Dreaming. We do not observe, but observations are based on a quantum-like interaction between everything else around us and ourselves. Dreaming is a knowing quality, which is beyond our personal identities and egos.

4. Process is a fourth level of consciousness including the other three. Awareness processes are a fourth-dimensional activity. They notice and can be part of Dreaming, dreams, and consensus reality, but are independent of any one of these realms. Awareness processes move in and out of the other three levels. The ability to notice experience is part of but also sometimes separate from the other three levels. All of these worlds are empirical; that is, they are real to the experiencer. Thus the awareness processes include the other levels and are real too, but this fourth domain notices the others. The meaning of this fourth domain will become more clear through the experiences brought forward by exercises in later chapters.

How to "Prove" a Theory about Dreams

The check on any theory about dreams, Dreamland, and Dreaming is the sum of our own observations and experiences that include our premonitions, tendencies, and everyday events. In other words, if you cannot experience or observe an interpretation as a *living fact,* that interpretation is incomplete. An empirical approach to dreams says that our dreamwork is valid when we can experience the origins and significance of a dream. If we cannot experience the interpretation, as a felt, lived, embodied reality, as a perception, then the interpretation is not complete.

The Nun's Story

Let me introduce another client of mine, a busy woman in her forties who consulted me because of chronic fatigue. When I asked her about her dreams, she told me she had dreamed about a nun called Anne. In the dream, my client was a child and Anne was very sensitive and kind to her.

According to my client, Anne was a very quiet woman, who was "connected to God." My client interpreted this dream to mean that she should be less extroverted and more inward in everyday life, that she should be more like Anne, who was one of her "shadow" figures. My client told me that Anne's behavior felt like the right manner in which to be self-caring, self-mothering.

That interpretation sounded fine to both of us, but to check it, I asked my client to notice what she was experiencing in the present moment of our session. She took a few moments, hesitated, and then said that there was "something weird, something like a slight tension in my jaws and throat." She told me that she had not really noticed that throat experience until that point in time when she was questioned. She thought the tension was not significant because it made no sense to her. She could not easily conceive a message or meaning in that tension.

I agreed that the tension might be insignificant, but then, it might be fun to know more about that tension, and I suggested focusing on it for another moment. She then said her tense throat felt as if her jaws were "pulling something inside." In other words, she experienced that cramp or tension as a sense of withdrawing in her throat.

As she followed this sense of withdrawing, she said she felt herself becoming quiet and heard a "subtle voice" saying, "Withdraw into yourself." Suddenly her intellectual interpretation, that she "should be less extroverted," made what she called, "body sense" to her because, as she said, she was "feeling and experiencing an interconnectedness with all things." She realized the meaning of her dream in terms of a body process—the tense throat—happening in the moment.

Figure 4. The Dreaming, not the dream, is central.

The psychological interpretation of the dream about Anne is centered in the framework of my client's everyday life; my client was too busy and extroverted and needed to establish a closer, more dedicated relationship to God. The spiritual interpretation is that she was a "hostess" to the Dreaming, that "something weird, something like a slight tension" in her jaws or throat, is unfolding the power of what Native Americans might call the "Great Spirit." From "Its" viewpoint, It is expressing Itself and unfolding into this world in terms of my client's throat tension, the dream of Anne, and her sense of tiredness in the midst of busy life.

The empirical attitude to dreamwork extends the older psychological method, which was readily satisfied with the intellectual understanding of dreams. The new dreamwork is based on access to and experience of altered states of consciousness. In the earlier methods, you could guess or speculate about the interpretation of a dream. One dream interpretation seems right, but another could be right as well. With the new method, there is one nonspeculative, evident interpretation: *the one you perceive and experience happening right now.*

Definitions

I have been using a number of terms so far. To make sure we understand one another, let me say what I mean by the use of certain terms, including those with the word "dream" in them:

Dreaming is the source of dreams; Dreaming is to dreams as a seed is to a plant. Dreaming is there before the plant grows. Dreaming is sentient, preverbal experience. While the "dream" that comes from Dreaming has parts and pictures, most of which are clear and which you can discuss, Dreaming is far less differentiated. It is a kind of nonverbal knowing, a sort of feeling or sense that was there *before the images or actions,* a feeling that expresses *it*self in terms of the psychological parts and their relationship to one another.

Lucid dreaming or *lucidity* occurs when you notice Dreaming tendencies happening in everyday life. Even before you are aware of an image or verbalizable content, you sense tendencies. Dreaming has no parts or pictures to It; yet if you are aware of It, that is, if you are lucid, you can unfold Its feeling or inclinations or tendencies into pictures, movement, dance, or anything else.

Dreamland is the world where Dreaming first expresses Itself, in a particular form such as the dualistic world of dreams, movement, dance, images, body aches and pains, and so on.

Dreams are verbalizable statements about a remembered but usually unintentional experience from the night or day, usually containing specific images, sounds, body feelings, smells, and so forth. Dreams are the first formulatable reflections your everyday mind makes of the almost unformulatable experiences of Dreaming. Dreams include the dream images from the night before, or those early morning memories of the night, the first song, mood, sentence, and fantasy you have while awakening in the morning. Dreams include sudden fears, feelings, and ideas that disturb your attention during the daytime.

Dreamwork relates the memories of Dreamland—namely, pictures, the images, fantasies, and body experiences—to the rest of your experience; that is, to everyday reality *and* the Dreaming.

- *Dreamwork relates dreams to everyday reality.* Dreamwork connects dream images to your identity, your age, your economics and health, your social situation, and so forth.

- *Dreamwork relates dreams to other events in Dreamland.* Dreamwork connects dreams to spontaneous, unintentional pictures, feelings, and thoughts. For example, dreamwork connected the remembered dream of Anne to (unintentional) throat tensions.

- *Dreamwork relates dreams to Dreaming,* the origins of perception. For example, in the previous discussion of the dream about the nun, the dreamwork consisted of relating pictures of the night, such as Anne, to perceptions of sensations and nonverbal feelings that were happening in the immediate moment.

Process work is a more general term than "dreamwork." Whereas dreamwork focuses on dreams from the night, process work focuses on the dreaming process that occurs night and day in individuals, couples, large groups, and people in coma, near death, or in psychotic or other extreme states. Process work is an attitude of respect for the unintentional and the unknown in all channels.[13]

Everyone Dreams

By including the Dreaming realm, I will be able to increase the application of dreamwork in later chapters to include people who do not remember dreams or who are not interested in their night-time dreams.

We now know that everyone dreams. Studies on people in their sleep state have revealed "rapid eye movements" (REMs): the minute motions the eyelids make while the person is asleep and dreaming. Waking people during these REMs resulted in reports that they were having dreams. Babies and people near death are apparently dreaming as well because they show REM activity just like everybody else. By the same measure, we know that dogs dream. My dog used to lick her lips when she was dreaming. After she awoke, she used to run out to get a bone I left for her. Cats dream too. Perhaps all animals dream. I guess that just about everything that is breathing is Dreaming and has dreams.

There seems to be no age limit to dreaming; we dream our entire lives.

---

[13]See my *River's Way* for more on the channels of perception.

No one has yet been able to say exactly what dreams are. I had a hard time finding a satisfying definition of dreams or dreamwork in the literature. There must be close to 150 books on dreams that you can buy in a large, big-city bookstore. But no one seems to say *what* a dream is. It was very surprising for me to go into Powell's Bookstore (the largest in Portland, Oregon) and find out that some dreamwork books quote me on what a dream is. Until now, I could not define what a dream is. Therefore, I was amazed to find myself being quoted as an authority. To me, this is an indication that, despite the antiquity of dreamwork, there still is little known about it. We have various methods of working with dreams, but little fundamental knowledge about their psychophysical nature.

As I said in chapter 1, there are many perspectives through which to view the unknown, from the viewpoints of Taoism, Buddhism, Hinduism, Aboriginal traditions, Judeo-Christian and Islamic traditions, and mystic traditions across the board to those of quantum physics and modern psychology.

Dreaming and the unknown were the center of the lives of our ancestors. For most of us living today, the center of life is our ordinary identity in our everyday, consensus reality. Our ordinary identity is a great identity, but it is all tied up with what we do, with success and failure, and with our ordinary thoughts and beliefs. To interpret dreams from that everyday framework is very valuable work that creates, finds meaning, and supports our ordinary way of making sense of our world.

Understanding dreams based on perception of subtle tendencies originating in altered states of consciousness gives another viewpoint about the Dreammaker's Mind. This viewpoint senses that the essence, or some primal mist, spontaneously creates all the rest of our experiences, observations, and acts.

Now we have at least two viewpoints about dreams. We can see things from our ordinary viewpoint or from that of the Dreaming perspective. We should know which viewpoint we are using, which reality we are tuning into. To identify with only consensus reality is tiring and eventually even depressing because only half of us is present. As we go on with this awareness training, a shift will occur in our attention as it detaches from everyday reality. You will identify with that uncanny and awesome source, the Dreaming, which makes life consistently worthwhile and dreams easier to understand.

 Things to Remember

1. Everyday reality, Dreamland, and Dreaming are intersecting worlds. Dreamwork focuses on all three worlds.

2. You can see the world from your ordinary everyday viewpoint or from that of the Dreammaker's essence.

3

The Dreammaker's Democracy

The ancient Buddhist text *Abhidhamma* has been very helpful to me for exploring how subtle experience from the Dreaming realm manifests in everyday awareness. This book of "higher teaching," as it is called, contains a detailed and scientific understanding of the nature of perception. If you are interested in perception, dreams, and Dreaming, you must know about this book! It says that anything you observe, every perception, has at least seventeen different steps to it. If you study and train your own perceptual processes, you will be able to differentiate seventeen different stages or more of perception.

From the time something in me intends to look out the window in my office to the moment I actually look through the window, there are between seventeen and forty-five perceptual acts. In the simplest formulation, there are seventeen "moments"; in the most complicated, there are forty-five different segments of perception according to ancient teaching. Most of us in average states of mind do not notice this level of perception. But we are no longer talking about the "average" everyday mind; we are talking about training the mind to notice subtle altered states of consciousness.

According to the teachings of the *Abhidhamma,* if you understand that what you experience arises and falls away, if you understand that this arising and falling away of perception happens without your doing anything, you will be able to detach from any event because you know that all things come and go. Things just happen. No one does them! In a way, no one is responsible for anything in Dreaming, and besides that, it is not you who perceives events.

You may have thought that *you* perceive things, but in fact, if you are trained in noticing how feelings, sensations, and observations arise and fall, you will notice that, to begin with, in the stage of Dreaming, perception just happens.

Buddhism As a Process

When you explore the basic elements of your awareness in meditation, you can see that your primary process—that is, your ordinary identity or the "little you"—is really a *product* of awareness and not the origin of it. The awareness process reveals that the Dreammaker creates myriad forms of expressions, one of which is the "little you," another of which is your dog; still others include the birds in your backyard and the lawn in the front. All the things you call your gifts and your problems are created by It, the awesome creative inner force I have been referring to as the "Dreammaker."

Consider the following example of perception that occurred to me while I was in the process of awakening one morning in Portland. There I was, sleeping in bed next to Amy; I was snoring. Then promptly at 6:30 A.M. outside our apartment, outside the bedroom, a huge clank occurred. It was Monday morning and the garbage truck was picking up junk.

This is a straightforward description of events—but only from the viewpoint of consensus reality! You could have videotaped these events. However, my Dreaming and dreams had another viewpoint. While the snoring and the clank were happening, I was still more or less asleep and experienced things other than everyday reality.

At first, as far as I can remember, I noticed something like a sound, but could not yet quite call it a "sound." All I know is that whatever was happening was no longer perceived by me as deep sleep. My awareness story proceeds in stages from the world of Dreaming into Dreamland's dreams. In the Dreaming stage, something is noticed. You couldn't quite say that I *noticed* anything, only that something is noticed. Then, in the next Dreamland state, I vaguely remember some sort of music occurring. Cymbals were clanking and clashing. They made a big noise. Clash, clank. Still in a dreamlike state, I witnessed an incredible symphony. Great music. Then, for some reason, something else occurred and I found my body getting up, sitting on the edge of my bed. I noticed that the window was open, and for some reason, I looked outside.

It was then that I finally heard noises outside, and suddenly realized the noise came from a garbage truck. This realization came after a series of processes. At first, I used my most lucid attention and noticed that something very subtle was happening to my perception. That happening began the waking up process.

But then finally, in my waking mind's eye, something decided the garbage truck was more important than the cymbals, the music, and that earliest something which began the whole process. Something in me sort of said to me, "Forget that dream about the cymbals, the music. That's all a bunch of dream stuff, it's not meaningful. Forget that essence that came before the music. The real thing is the garbage truck, go back to sleep or get up, but whatever you do, it's okay to forget the music and the essence." As a result, I had to work to remember my dream and the essence that preceded it.

This whole perceptual process that I just described occurring to me in the morning in Portland actually happened in a few seconds of real time, the kind of time you can measure with your watch. However, these seconds were wondrous and crucial moments in my life. In the first moments of the Dreaming, before even noticing the cymbals, the Buddhist *Abhidhamma* would say that seven differentiable stages of perception occurred. I described those first moments with only a few sentences about some early stage of awakening. Nevertheless, trained meditators can notice many little steps happening in their perception.

The stage extending from deepest sleep to the existence of a dream is what I have been calling "the Dreaming," or *sentient perception*. Something in my body knows things in this stage, yet the person I refer to as "Arny" was not yet present.

Sentient perception is preverbal, nondualistic experience. Sentient perception is part of the Dreaming realm, the first realm in figure 5.

As you can see in the figure, in the split second after the first seven stages, another seven appear, stages eight to fourteen in the *Abhidhamma* system. I call the second realm "Dreamland," where an "I" appears. In Dreamland, I am having a dream in which there are cymbals and music. I am in the world of parts, of duality. "I" appear and begin to think to myself that there are cymbals clashing. It seems to me that I hear a symphony. Since I am lucid at this point, I notice that my musical dream happened after that original disturbance in which there was a sentient experience of no longer being in deep sleep.

Perception unfolds itself and finally, I arrive at realm three, Everyday Reality (*Abhidhamma*'s stages fifteen to seventeen), where I get out of bed, go to the window, and see the garbage truck. I now think that the garbage truck is "real" and everything else is a dream. And so I forget and marginalize what occurred in Dreamland and in Dreaming in favor of reality (see figures 6 and 7).

Stages of Perception	1 2 3 4 5 6 7	8 9 10 11 12 13 14	15 16 17
Realm of Perception	**1. Dreaming**	**2. Dreamland**	**3. Everyday Reality**
What is perceived	Sentient, preverbal experience	Duality, Dreamland's parts	Memory of parts
Awareness experience	Lucidity about Dreaming	Awareness of dreams	Consciousness of everyday reality
Filtering out awareness experience	Marginalization	Edges	Repression

Figure 5. Stages of perception.

Figure 6. Consensus reality: the garbage truck.

Figure 7. Dreamland: clashing of musical cymbals.

Everyone experiences these seventeen stages, although we may not be used to tracking observations with such preciseness. Why are we so attached to the different worlds when we are in them—to Dreamland and then to consensus reality? Why do we love to be in deep sleep and Dreaming, believe so much in our dreams while in Dreamland, and then become so attached to consensus reality when we are awake? Why do we believe that each reality is all there is when we are in it, and tend to forget the rest? When we are in the

Dreaming, it is all-important. When we are in Dreamland, we forget the Dreaming from which dreams come. By the time we're awake, we forget most of our dreams, the music, and our Dreaming.

Something in us encourages us to forget where the dreams came from. I almost said "we" make this choice, but that's really not quite right. Something in us, in Dreamland, chooses not to notice or chooses to marginalize the original disturbances that happened in Dreaming. Then, when we are back in consensus reality, something marginalizes or forgets the symphony so that the garbage truck is, finally, just a garbage truck, and not music.

Something marginalizes unwanted, uncomfortable perceptions. Unless you are a highly trained meditator, experiences of the Dreaming get marginalized without your awareness in the earliest stages of perception. This is how personality is created. Something keeps out events and impressions that do not make sense or fit, so these impressions are ignored. For example, at a given moment, while lying in bed, slight weird, wavelike sensations may be marginalized because they just don't fit the stable impression we have of lying in bed. At another point, impulsive energies or even fatigue may be marginalized. In any case, by the time you have the impression of having a dream in Dreamland, there is a you and a not-you. Something—your body or the Dreammaker of the universe—marginalizes the sentient interactions preceding dreams.

Such marginalization is probably responsible for making Western therapists focus on dreams instead of the Dreaming, for dreams, with their identifiable parts and associations, are closer to consensus reality.

What is the greater purpose behind the Dreammaker's marginalizing subtle, sentient experience? I don't know. I don't even know if such questions coming from consensus reality about the Dreaming can be answered in a linear, reasonable manner. I only know for sure that the Dreammaker's Dreaming tends to unfold in terms of parts and worlds that forget one another. I also know for sure that without dreams, we would have no sense of relativity about our consensus reality. We need dreams and the Dreaming to observe the everyday world. Likewise, without consensus reality and dreams, Dreaming could never know itself. Life would simply be a constant flow. Perhaps there would only be God-intoxicated states, and no "one" to appreciate these states of being. Perhaps the Dreammaker loves creating individual dream parts, life-forms, people, and objects, to know Itself in infinite detail and endless permutations.[14]

In any case, Dreaming creates personality. Every moment, something is dreaming you up by marginalizing the unitary world, making you feel as if there is a *you,* and everything else is not-*you* or nonexistent. Dreaming, the Aboriginal Dreamtime, gets marginalized. And then you can only imagine yourself to be this single, solitary person.

However, if you meditate and expand your awareness, you notice that, actually, you and all "your" thoughts are not created by you. You know that you arise, you are created, and your thoughts arise. Suddenly you get the impression that Dreaming is the real thing, not you! You are an illusion created by Dreaming and Its temporary marginalization of everything else as not-you. That is why I am saying that to understand anything about yourself, and especially about your dreams, you need access to Dreaming and to that grand and incomprehensible essence, the Dreammaker. This cosmic intelligence makes me think I am a person by forgetting Itself.

In my *Quantum Mind,* I point out that the universe's laws and principles—you might say its "plan" at this point in evolution—seems to be to expand, to differentiate itself into parts. That is why

---

[14]This idea that God created the world to know Herself or Himself is found in many mystics' belief systems, including Jung's *Answer to Job,* and the works of Rainer Maria Rilke and William Blake.

there is a *you* and an *I,* six billion times over on this planet, and more in this universe. The universe expands into its multitude of parts and then, theoretically, will contract again back to Dreaming. The physics of this process is speculative and has not been proven, but meditation and perception can be experienced now in Dreamland and Dreaming. Your daily experience shows that you forget the dreaming mind and get fascinated by yourself as a single person. And then at night, you contract, so to speak, and go back to dreaming.

The Buddhists teach that once you know you are arising out of the void, you can detach from yourself and the events of everyday life. That's when you can laugh like a Zen master. When you are close to the Dreaming, the most serious things about this world seem funny and unnecessarily important. Then with your original natural mind, your open or beginner's mind, your Buddha nature, you see the different realities clearly: Dreaming, Dreamland, and everyday reality.

With lucidity you notice how the Dreammaker reflects on Itself and parts emerge; one of these parts is you. Then the little you is firmed up, so to speak, by marginalizing the Dreaming. Once you are a firm and set personality, the little you continues by making sure that everything that is not-you remains that way. You are *not* the teacher if you are a student. Then, when you are the teacher, you are *not* the student.

This reminds me of a two-year-old child with whom I recently worked. We were sitting on the floor playing, and at one point I began to act like a baby. When I played with her as if I were a baby, she clearly said to me, "Arny, No! You are a man. You are *not* a baby!" In her mind, she was the baby, since she was two, and I was the man! We were not one another. That is how this universe unfolds into parts and keeps them separate.

The worlds of consensus reality and Dreamland are created similarly. In the Buddhist teachings, if you get to know yourself really well, you will be able to notice the sentient level and know that you can choose not to marginalize it. You know that at some level there is no you or I, there is only an "It."

In practice, your tendency to marginalize experience happens at the sentient level. If you are lucid about sentient experience, you can catch this happening and reverse it. You can predict dream figures by noticing how they arise. Dream figures are faces of sentient experience. Dreams point back to Dreaming.

When your awareness is open, you are aware of the sentient level of experience, of marginalization at this level, and of valuing Dreamland and consensus reality. Such awareness would be a form of "enlightenment," by which I mean being lucid of the Dreaming and being conscious of parts, all at the same time.

In the example of the garbage truck, I was in a rare and lucid mood. Something in me noticed my sleep being disturbed. And I was also aware of that disturbance appearing in the world of parts as music in Dreamland. Then I noticed how that disturbance appeared in consensus reality as a garbage truck. But even while I was looking at the garbage truck, I was still vaguely aware that some unfathomable, mysterious Dreaming created that garbage truck and that symphony.

That mystery wanted to see itself in terms of music and garbage. Then I almost forgot it all. My point is that the dream itself is a final expression of something that has already had quite a history of arising.

Marginalization and Edges

Marginalization happens before there is even an "I." By the time you perceive that *you* are observing not-you parts, there is a barrier, an "edge" between you and everything else. You have the experience that they are separate from you.

The difference between edges and marginalization is that marginalization is sentient and goes on without an I. Edges require an I. From the viewpoint of the Dreaming realm, without training you arise and Dreaming is forgotten. This forgetting is what I mean by marginalization. Marginalization helps to create your particular personality and the perception of other things that are deemed not-you. Marginalization makes you think that your thoughts are yours as a single, solitary entity.

The analogy of a theater can be used to explain more about the Dreammaker's marginalizing tendency. In the theater, someone must be in the background to make the curtain come down. And someone must work the spotlights. There is an audience that comes to the theater to be entertained. In a way, the Dreammaker creates the theater, the stage, the objects and people of everyday life. The Dreammaker's tendencies direct the theater spotlight to focus on certain things and marginalize others. Although the Dreammaker is not a person, we can imagine It to be a person holding the spotlight on the stage.

The analogy of the spotlight gives a sense of how specifically our attention is focused. The spotlight shines on only one section of the stage, and the rest of the people, parts, and roles are left in the shadows or the margins. In other words, marginalization happens when the spotlight focuses solely on particular actors, ignoring everyone else in the theater.

In this way, you can be an observer in the audience and enjoy the play, focusing on one scene or actress at a time. In a similar way, we are observers watching events in Dreamland or reality, ignoring the existence of the theater itself, with its many aspects, including the Dreammaker who is running the whole thing. Marginalization happens before there's even a person to come to the theater. The Dreammaker marginalizes through Its use of the spotlight! (See figure 8.)

Figure 8. The Dreammaker focuses attention by paying attention to one figure or scene and marginalizing the rest.

When the Dreammaker—let's say the Mind of God—puts you in the spotlight, you sit in the audience and see yourself in a dream. In this way you become separated from everything else and you become a person in a body at a certain time and space. For example, "Arny" is one of the roles the Dreammaker created. Another role might be you.

Now, once you are in the play or watching it, you may feel that certain other people or events should not be in that play. Since there is a you, we can speak of you having an "edge." You may want to forget certain figures and events in that play, or even the whole play, the dream itself. Thus, while marginalization happens at the deepest level of awareness, edges are closer to your ordinary, everyday psychology. Edges are what make you undemocratic towards certain figures and parts of yourself. You don't feel they deserve representation in your life.

As you develop your lucidity, you remember the Dreammaker expressing Itself through everything and everyone. Lucidity helps you value everyone involved in this theater. You know everyone is needed for the play, everything is a potentially significant, if momentary, role in the whole show of life. Even though the Dreammaker marginalizes some experiences including Itself at one time or another, in time, with lucidity, you can notice this happening and even reverse it, if you so choose.

The Ways of the Dreammaker

The Dreammaker, the Big You, has countless names. It was called the Goddess Nun by the early Egyptians; the Creator of Things; Shiva, Brahma, or Shakti by the Hindus; Pan Ku by the Chinese; Buddha Mind by the Buddhists; Allah by the Moslems; Yahweh by the Jews; Christ by the Christians. The Dreammaker works in multitudinous ways, but creation is part of all of them.

For example, early Egyptians believed that the Goddess Nun created individual life-forms out of the indivisible sea. The Hindus believed that the energy of Shakti, their primordial mother, created all living things. In quantum physics, it is thought that the very intention to observe brings forth elementary particles out of formless quantum wave fields.

In normal states of consciousness, you focus only on what is central on the stage and normally do not pay attention to the audience or to who is holding the spotlight. Dreaming is marginalized; the Dreammaker marginalizes Itself. Perhaps that is why people have always wondered about the source of life and worried about its ending in "death." Fear is caused by not knowing the eternal part of yourself, the Dreammaker. If we saw the source of life, the Dreammaker, we might tend to be less fearful.

Once we have contact with the Dreammaker and Its Dreaming, everything is easier. Then you can become the Dreammaker's apprentice, and learn to sense the Dreammaker train your ordinary mind to notice incomprehensible sensations and signals from an invisible source. Some call this source "nature," "love," or "community." You cannot see any of these things or prove they exist; you cannot measure them. Yet you sense their existence. And you can sense yourself becoming Its apprentice.

The Earthquake

Because feelings and sensations of Dreaming are marginalized, it is sometimes difficult to figure out what is happening with you during a time when you sense that you have a problem. Something feels out of kilter. But if you ask yourself, "What's my problem?" you may not be able to describe exactly what the problem is. You have a problem; you know that. But what is it? Because of marginalization, the details of your problem do not appear. For example, you may feel depressed and still not know the source of your depression. If you spend enough time getting to the basic roots, to the dreaming essence of the experience of the depression, it solves itself.

Consider the following example. One of my clients complained that he frequently feels ill. All he could say was that he is chronically depressed at the end of each day. He had no detailed description of that depression and could not figure out why he felt that way. He had gone to every possible doctor and healer without much success.

He said that his outer life was just fine; he was moderately successful and, according to him, had every reason to be happy. The chief executive officer in his organization had just died, and he was being asked to take that job. My client felt excited about that, but also said he felt that he might be too young to do this work.

After telling me about his successful life, he grudgingly agreed to focus on the feeling of being depressed. When I asked him how it felt to be depressed, he could not really answer. All he could say was that the depression always began with a feeling of being slightly nauseated. With some encouragement, I suggested he follow that feeling, pretending it was here *now*. He was hesitant, but after a while, pretended he felt nauseous. Soon he really was!

Instead of marginalizing the discomfort of the nausea, he decided to courageously feel those unwanted, nauseating sensations. He said they scared him, he feared throwing up. After a few minutes of concentration on his experience, he broke out in a sweat and whispered that he felt a "rumbling," not in his stomach, but beneath his feet. He said this was crazy to feel, but it seemed to him as if the ground was moving. He had sensations that gave him the experience of an earthquake.

He asked if he was having a panic attack, and I assured him all this would clarify itself soon enough and that he should have courage and just follow the proceedings (of this Dreaming) with his best attention. He was afraid but went on. He insisted things were not getting better but worse. In fact, he experienced that rumble as a sort of fantasy that this was not a simple earthquake but that the whole world was ending.

He asked what all this was bringing him; things were worse, not better, and more mysterious than ever. What a crisis we were in—the end of the world! Briefly said, he allowed himself to focus on that rumbling, that earthquake. Soon the world crumbled and disappeared, and we (I was now part of the imagery) ended up floating in outer space. He shocked himself, discovering that in his fantasy of outer space, he was no longer nauseated or afraid but actually loved floating out there. He confessed to me that, to his own surprise, he felt a lot better in outer space than on Earth!

When he looked down from outer space, the Earth came into view, and he, after some hesitation, decided to return to the world. But to his great surprise, he imagined he landed in a cave in the mountains. He loved it there, detached from his everyday life. He cried with happiness and realized a new part of his life was now beginning. He called this part his "cave." He decided he wanted to be "in his cave," in the sense of being inwardly quiet, even when at work. He was thrilled with this possibility. His depression disappeared and instead, he remained in the quietude of his cave as much as possible, especially in his work.

Now let's go back to his problem of depression. What was his problem? Did he have a biological or chemical problem? Did he have too little support from his parents? Was he having a midlife crisis and fearing growing older? Analyze the situation as you like. From the empirical viewpoint, he was trying to ignore his depression and marginalize the sensation of nausea. As he focused on the nausea, it turned out that he was feeling queasy because of an imagined rumbling earthquake. The Dreaming was trying to catch his attention through depression, through nausea, and then by shaking up his world and throwing him into outer space and into an inner cave. In other words, what he called a depression was the *beginning* of a dreaming process that unfolded into a sense of inwardness.

With my encouragement and support, my client stopped marginalizing his experiences and calling them "depression," and instead, focused on the Dreaming. He went into sensations he did not like, went further into rumblings of the ground, into a sort of panic-stricken abyss. After that, the Dreaming unfolded into the outer-space experience, where he felt delightfully detached from the world.

The night after we worked together, he had another dream. This time, he dreamed about oysters. He told me he knew immediately what that was about. Oysters were like a cave; pearls lie buried in oysters, just as valuable experiences were imbedded in the inner cave he had been ignoring.

From a purely perceptual viewpoint, perhaps the only problems we have are the result of marginalization and edges.

Deep Democracy in Dreaming

The point is that the Dreaming (in the form of sensations like fatigue and nausea) unfolds into figures and parts and images. In the example I just described, the Dreaming unfolded into images such as outer space, a cave on Earth, business, and even oysters. If you marginalize Dreaming, you are no longer grounded in the basic process that is trying to occur to you. Grounding means sensing the Dreaming, becoming the Dreammaker's apprentice.

In figure 9, the Dreaming is at the base of the cone and center of the circle. The Dreaming unfolds like a flower with various "petals." The sentient realm comprises the roots, and out of the sentient roots grow different parts of the dream.

Normally, the Dreammaker Itself rarely appears in dreams; you rarely see the figure holding the spotlight; you don't often see God in an anthropomorphic form. Yet, from the perspective of the Dreammaker, all dream events and figures are parts of It—they are Its grand theater: the Dreammaker is somewhere on or off stage.

It seems that over time, the Dreammaker is deeply democratic. It treats all Its creations, all Its images and sensations as equally valuable and needed. That attitude is what I mean by "deep democracy." It appreciates the nausea, the pearl, the earthquake, and the boss as all-important features of life.

Although you and I value one person, event, object over another, apparently the Dreammaker's attitude is that all experiences and parts are important. This kind of democracy is present in everyone, even when our little selves feel unbalanced, even crazy. Deep down, the Dreammaker is still there, using all our "good" and "bad" experiences to express Itself in Its grand theater.

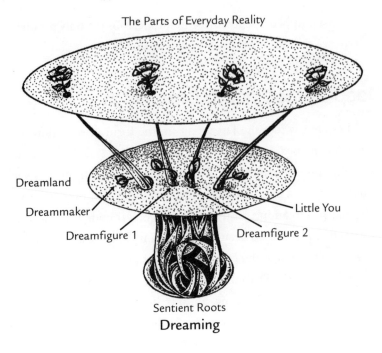

The Parts of Everyday Reality

Dreamland

Dreammaker

Dreamfigure 1

Little You

Dreamfigure 2

Sentient Roots

Dreaming

Figure 9: How the Dreaming unfolds.

However, valuing each level of consciousness and each particular aspect of every level is not the only way in which the Dreammaker's deep democracy seems to manifest. After working for many years with many different kinds of dreamers, it seems to me that the Dreammaker is deeply democratic in the way various viewpoints are presented in any given series of fragments.

For example, it often seems as if one dream fragment comes from your point of view, then another fragment appears that represents the view of someone opposed to you. Still a third fragment of a dream may represent the viewpoint of the Dreammaker, without such an intelligence actually appearing as a figure in the dream. In other words, deep democracy appears to create the viewpoints of the various dream fragments.

In any case, when we are not aware of the Dreammaker, we tend to interpret our dreams from our own viewpoint or the viewpoint of one of the other figures. Then we end up with psychological prescriptions, criticisms, or praises. "You need to do this, do that, become aware of this or that, and so forth." We end up excited or depressed. We interpret our dreams from the viewpoint of the boss, or the depression, or the cave, or the oyster, and forget that all of these viewpoints are important, but that any one viewpoint is not enough.

If you are close to the Dreammaker, however, you see yourself and the dream events as parts of the incredible unfolding of the theater called "this world," including all your body experiences and everyone and everything you know. From Its viewpoint, the little you and the little me calling one another good and bad are all necessary parts of this grand theater. All of us are needed to see the various faces of God. We can't prove this, but we can surely sense it.

 ## Things to Remember

1. Perception happens, Dreaming unfolds into dreams and consensus reality—including garbage trucks.

2. The Dreammaker is deeply democratic. Although It focuses the spotlight on one level of reality or on one of Its figures at any given moment, over time It seems to treat all of Its figures and experiences as equally important.

4

The Dreammaker's Breath

In the preceding three chapters of this book, I discussed how the Dreaming inspires everything else into being. You sense this Dreaming working through your subtle tendencies, moods, sensations, sounds, smells, pressures, and so forth. I have pointed out that the meaning of a dream can be experienced most dramatically through having a sense of this Dreaming. Learning to sense the Dreaming makes us the Dreammaker's apprentices, so to speak.

We have discussed that, while the experience of Dreaming is preverbal, Dreamland has identifiable parts. For example, there is a *you* and an *I* unfolded out of the Dreaming. The parts of Dreamland are virtual; only *you,* the dreamer, see or feel or experience them. You cannot show them to anyone else. *You* can see your dream image, but no one else sees the same thing as long as their consciousness is focused solely on consensus reality.

In the Dreamland, what we call space is actually spacelike and cannot be measured and shared with someone else—unless he or she is in the same deep altered state of consciousness that you are in. For example, you can dream you travel hundreds of miles, but these miles are not the kind you can measure in consensus reality. You may feel while you are dreaming that it took you hours to do this or that. This timelike sense, however, is not a consensus reality form of time that can be measured with a watch. Dreamland's space and time are precursors of our sense of space and time in consensus reality.

In consensus reality, the parameters of time and space that we experience as absolutes are actually perceived that way only by agreement. When you speak of an event at four o'clock, everyone knows what you are talking about. "Consensus" reality is everyday life. Its parts are not virtual; they are "real"—which is to say, they are believed to constitute reality.[15]

In a fourth level of awareness, in the process level of awareness, you can be lucid about the tendencies in Dreaming; you also sense how you move into and out of Dreamland into everyday consensus reality. In figure 10, I have assembled the various realms and summarized typical awareness experiences characteristic of these realms. In the chart, "NCR" stands for nonconsensus reality and "CR" stands for consensus reality.

The Figures and Parts of Dreams

To understand how the figures in Dreamland come about, it is helpful for me to think of dream figures in terms of the patterns you might see on a sandy beach. Have you ever noticed that when the water from the sea hits the land, it splashes and leaves a pattern on a sandy beach? Likewise, when Dreaming meets your everyday identity,

---

[15]The absoluteness of the consensual ideas of space and time was relativized by Albert Einstein in his relativity theory. He showed that measurement of distance and extension in time depend on the framework from which a measurement takes place.

Dreaming leaves patterns "on the beach," some of which you call the figures in your dreams. In this analogy, the beach is the border, Dreamland, where the Dreaming meets your everyday reality. Thus the Dreaming appears as a bunch of patterns or players in Dreamland.

Now, the beach is a good analogy for patterns, but not for the way in which these patterns interact. We need to think of the beach, that is Dreamland, as a stage and the patterns as players on that stage. It seems as if there are usually three or four major roles or players in your dreams creating an amazing nightly theater. Take a moment and think about the typical players in your dreams. Write out the cast of figures that frequently act in your inner theater. Getting to know yourself or someone else means knowing your, his, and/or her players. For example, there may be a role for the inner critic, occupied by different people in your life.

When you bring together in your mind's eye the various roles such as the opponent, ally, teacher, spook, and so on, Dreamland seems to be a kind of group process. In fact, dreams often seem as if they are a group process searching for a facilitator who knows what is happening!

To recognize your cast of figures, to understand how they arise out of the Dreaming and what their meaning might be in your everyday life, try the following training exercise.

Dreamwork Exercise. The Four Levels of Dreaming

The purpose of all the exercises in this book is to help you in your apprenticeship with the Dreammaker. Its Dreaming is one of your greatest, if not the greatest, teacher. Make yourself comfortable wherever you are sitting or lying or standing (if you are in a subway). This exercise is more effective if you take notes, so have a pencil and a piece of paper nearby.

Figure 10.
Awareness realms.

1. Dreaming

Awareness of vague
tendencies
Awareness of being
without parameters
such as time or space

2. Dreams + Dreamworld

Awareness of separate
parts and people
Awareness of NCR time
and space

3. Consensus Reality

Awareness of CR
events and everyday life
Awareness of CR time and
space

4. Process

Awareness of the level
events occur in
Awareness of levels and
changing levels

1. **Choose a dream to work on.** Recall a dream you have had; any dream that comes to mind will do, but if possible, choose a recent, preferably short dream. Choose *one* dream that you'd like to investigate, to know more about. Please jot it down now.

2. **Dream figures.** Think about that dream, or even a fragment of the dream. Who or what were the main players? Describe a couple of them. Even if the dream is a little vague, recall one or two characters or parts. That's all you have to do with the dream at this point. Note those characters or parts.

3. **Breathing.** Now put your dream aside and concentrate on your breathing. If your mind allows you to do this, use counting to focus your attention. Count each time you exhale up to the number ten, then start again. Breathing out, you will count "one"; breathing out, you count "two"; and so on. Just notice how you breathe; hear your breath, feel its rise and fall, follow it. Keep going until you have reached the number ten or have the sense that your mind is concentrated and emptier, perhaps quieter than usual. This technique takes practice, so take the time now to practice following your body's own natural method of breathing. You don't have to change your breath, just notice it.

4. **Notice tendencies.** When you feel settled in the rhythm of your breathing, notice sentient experiences; that is, any slight sensations or micromovements that seem to want to be focused on. Your unconscious mind will know which tendency or sensation to focus on. Use your attention to notice the subtlest experience. Even if it's unfamiliar to you, keep your attention on the sensation, notice it, and don't let go of your awareness. Make a note about this sensation and ask yourself why you have not noticed it until now. If you have been marginalizing this sensation, how come?

5. **Notice and unfold this sensation.** When you're ready, let this sentient experience give rise to more explicit sensations, and finally to images of these sensations in your mind's eye. In other words, let the slight sensation or sentient experience produce images, even sounds or motions, if you like. (If focusing on sensations in this manner is new for you, imagine you are a child having these sensations. Let your childlike creativity unfold these sensations in a cartoonlike manner.) When you are ready, let that sentient experience express itself in terms of figures or sounds. How many figures arise? One? Two? Make a note of these figures. Catch and note them!

6. **Edges and democracy.** How are these figures the same as or different from you? Do you feel that you are better than or worse than these figures? Do you feel that you are more significant or less significant than they are, in your own mind?

   If you feel that you are either better or worse than these figures, you are creating edges and barriers to them. Explore the possibility that the figures are equally significant and you are equally significant with all the rest of these figures. Just experiment with that possibility. All are equally important. Experiment with becoming compassionate and opening to the various cultures and behaviors inside yourself.

   Notice and explore any communication between these figures, and you. Notice what, if any, sort of communication, even a brief interaction between you and these figures, occurs. Make a note about this interaction.

7. **Sentient experience compared with dream images.** Now let us reconsider your dream, the one you mentioned in step one. What are some of your associations with the dream figures? Do they remind you of something or someone? Now that you know your

associations, compare the figures that arose from your sentient experiences with the figure or figures in your dream. How are the figures the same? What if anything is different? What can you learn about your dream figures from the figures that came from your breathing experience, your sentient experience? Examining the connection possible between your sentient experiences and dream figures might give you a sense of the meaning of your dream.

8. **Dream interpretation in CR.** We shall soon ask about the relationship of your dream images to your everyday life. I call this the psychological interpretation of your dream. Then we shall be asking about your relationship to the Dreaming, the Dreammaker. I call this relationship, the spiritual interpretation of the Dream. We shall be looking at your experiences from the viewpoint that all of the figures are more or less equally significant.

   Psychological interpretation. Recall your sentient experience and how it connects to your dream. What is the significance of that dream for you right now? What could it mean for you in connection to events of your everyday life? What is the meaning of this experience for the next few hours and days? What significance could Dreaming and the dream have for your body? Your relationships? Your connection to your family or group? Make a note about all these things.

   Spiritual interpretation. To discover the spiritual background to your dream, recall the sentient experiences you just had and reexperience them. These sentient Dreaming tendencies are the source of your dreams and fantasies. Consider the possibility that you are a hostess or host for this Dreaming. Imagine that the Dreammaker is trying to express Itself, Its nature, through you. If you can, explore the possibility of switching identities and imagine that you yourself are not your ordinary self, but the Dreammaker. Pretend and imagine that You, the Dreammaker, are looking for a host or hostess through which you can express Yourself. Make a note of Your feelings and experiences as the Dreammaker.

9. **Process level.** Now notice where your attention is. Are you focusing on some of the images that have just come up? If so, note that you are focusing on Dreamland and just let your awareness follow the different experiences you're having. Just track them. Notice, "Now I am aware of this experience, now I notice that." Alternatively, are you focusing on the *tendencies* and subtle sensations you normally marginalize? If so, just note you are working with the Dreaming. Or are you thinking about *how to apply* all this in your everyday life? If so, notice you are focusing on consensus reality. Let your awareness track whether you are in Dreamland, the Dreaming, or consensus reality. Take a few minutes with this.

The point of this exercise is to train you in tracking your experiences, and to help you become the Dreammaker as well as Its apprentice. From your ordinary viewpoint, the interpretation of the dream is about your everyday reality. As you cultivate the deep democracy of the Dreaming—the attitude that *all* levels and parts are important, you also learn to appreciate the Dreammaker's level. From Its viewpoint, It is using the ordinary, everyday little you to express Itself.

Another point of this exercise is to become more lucid about the subtle tendencies within yourself. As you recognize these tendencies, you realize that your dreams are not totally mysterious. In fact, they become more understandable in terms of the preverbal feelings and sensations you normally marginalize.

An Example of Breathing Anxiety

A university student, a client of mine living overseas, had a dramatic experience when we worked on this exercise during a telephone session. She complained about feeling stuck in school. She said she just could not complete her exams. She did not know why. She told me she had dreamed about her partner, who was "a very courageous and strong woman who is capable of fixing things which are broken in the apartment." In the dream, her partner was fixing something in the apartment, and she was learning to do so as well.

I first attempted to interpret that dream with her in the old way. I said, "Well, perhaps you are growing to be as strong as your partner, and that strength will allow you to finish up your exams." She liked my interpretation but said, "I still felt stuck."

I then suggested that she follow her breathing experiences, after counting one to ten in the manner of the above exercise. After breathing and counting quietly to herself for some moments, she mumbled something about fear. "I am afraid of my breathing," she said. "It terrifies me, because I have a little asthma and focusing on my breath gets me in touch with a little tiny sense of feeling smothered. I have lung anxiety, it is as if someone angry is smothering or killing another person."

I told her I wished she had had a more pleasant experience, but suggested that she focus on the "killer" for a moment. In a flash she said, "I am fed up with myself, with my own reluctance to finish things up. I could kill myself, that lazy part of me which feels she does not have the intelligence to finish things up! My partner is always telling me, I should just finish those damn exams, and she is right!"

I said nothing, but listened as she energetically and enthusiastically said, "Okay, I'll do it!"

The psychological meaning of her dream, in which her partner was fixing something in the apartment and she was learning to do so as well, was to develop the strength her partner had. However, the sentient experience, those slight, smothering feelings, made her realize her own strength, and the fact that she was actually fed up with her own "reluctance to finish things up." She was not merely stuck, she was angry and full of energy. The Dreammaker wanted her to move on with her life!

Devilish Example

Another example of sentient work comes to mind, in which subtle experience gave a totally surprising dream interpretation. One of my readers who did this exercise told me she had dreamed she tried to kiss someone on the ear, but the person rejected her and left.

Figure 11. Dream of the attempted kiss.

When she did this exercise, she found that the sentient experience that appeared after meditating on her breath was a burning sensation in her back. When she focused on this and then let that sentient experience unfold, it became what she called a "passionate red color." This sensation and its red color then turned into a wild, devilish, fun, "sexy demon." She saw a playful but devilish creature looking at her (see figure 12).

Figure 12. Devilish creature: image emerging from sentient experience.

Suddenly the experience of that passionate redness and the image that emerged from it helped her understand her dream of trying to kiss someone and being rejected. She told me she was in a passionate, intense, devilish mood, and a part of her rejects that because this "part" is afraid her own devilish passion will get her into trouble in relationships.

How would you now interpret her dream of trying to kiss someone and getting rejected? Chances are you will say that she should accept her kissing and passionate nature. That would be an interesting psychological interpretation. But no, she found out something different. When she tried to see all parts as equally important—when she assumed the viewpoint of the Dreaming—

she decided that her devilish nature was wonderful *and* that the part of her that was against it was *also* important. She described the person rejecting her as "shy." The two parts of her belong together; shyness and passion are just different faces of her process!

For her, the correct psychological interpretation of her dream, which focuses on the framework of her everyday reality, is that she is trying to open up to her devilish, passionate nature, but her shyness is not quite ready. The spiritual interpretation is that passion and shyness are wanderers, looking for some dreamer to host them for the night. This surprising understanding came from the discovery of her passionateness *and* fear of it.

What You May Have Learned

The point is that our momentary, deep, unverbalized sentient experiences give us an empirical experience of our dreams. Because of our relationship to everyday reality, however, we tend to marginalize sentient experience of the Dreaming.

Dreaming is as universal as breathing. It is an almost imperceptible experience that goes on all the time, even when we are sleeping. It is subtle but can be detected by using awareness. Sentient experience is a mixture of voluntary and involuntary experience. We tend to marginalize breathing and Dreaming, taking them both for granted.

I suggest you follow the wisdom and subtle quality of breathing. Breathing just happens. When you work with yourself or someone else on dreams, *don't work,* let things happen. Using your awareness is the opposite of trying to change people. It's easier and usually more sustainable to use awareness. If you simply use awareness instead of telling somebody how he or she should change, you are not working against the grain of the present state of consciousness and your work—which isn't really dream "work" anymore—will be easier.

Any suggestion, however brilliant or well-meaning, that directs the person to do anything more than noticing his or her subtle tendencies will not hold for more than a few hours. Using your awareness to notice how you marginalize subtle events—that is, becoming more lucid about the Dreaming—will allow you to comprehend the background from which dreams occur.

Things to Remember

1. To understand your dreams, start by noticing the sentient experiences or tendencies and sensations that are normally marginalized.

2. Don't work at dreamwork; think of it as an awareness practice instead.

3. Remember, all parts and experiences are important.

2

CO-CREATIVE DREAMING

How to Interpret Dreams
Using Altered States

5

Symbols Are Twigs
That Sprout Roots

In part 2, I will discuss the theory and practice of a new process technique I call "co-creative Dreaming." The reason that I'm using the term "co-creative" for this particular aspect of process work is because the prefix "co-" means "together." The dreamer, together *with the interpreter, co-*creates the dream's meaning by entering into the altered state of consciousness, the Dreaming together. Of course, everything we do is co-creative because of the interactions between all things in Dreaming. However, this co-creativity is usually marginalized. As a technique, however, co-creative Dreaming is not just implicitly or mildly co-creative; it is explicitly co-creative.

This method is applicable for working on yourself (that is, for your everyday mind working with Dreaming) without outside assistance or, as stated, for working with another dreamer's dreams. In the new dreamwork method, you are not just one wise woman or man understanding (yourself or) the other person; there is a real partnership involved, and both of you will be invited to enter into altered states of consciousness.

Review

In part 1, I spoke of the *Abhidhamma,* which explicates the ancient Buddhist tradition of understanding perception in terms of various stages. Remember my example about waking up in the morning and noticing that noisy garbage truck?

At first, all I knew was that something was disturbing me; that sense of disturbance was the sentient part of the experience. Then suddenly I heard a symphony, and musical cymbals were clashing, making noises. This music was part of Dreamland. And then the perceptual process unfolded further as I went to the window and I realized that in consensus reality, the disturbance or music was "just" a garbage truck. Then I marginalized the other Dreaming and Dreamland experiences and stood squarely in consensus reality.

I remind you of that example to underscore the perceptual training needed to catch these subtle perceptions and tendencies of Dreaming. Such training helps you to *know* that dreams are linked empirically with sentient experience.

As I stated in part 1, you are constantly Dreaming through four worlds. The first is the sentient world of "I-less" perception; the second is Dreamland, in which the little you appears as one of the figures in dreams. In Dreamland the larger you, or You, is the community of parts. The third world is that of consensus, everyday reality, the world of the garbage truck; the fourth is the ever-changing state of awareness that moves through but is none of these worlds.

Consensus reality is a place where you are more or less fixedly established in terms of your family and relationships, your studies, work, retirement, and so forth. What is your work? What is your relationship to school, business, and religious community? To your friends?

Consensus reality strongly influences dreams. The time of year and the location a dreamer is living in are important pieces of information about the dreamer's consensus reality. Where do you live? What are the social and political issues of your area? What is the geography surrounding you? What season is it? The seasons can have a significant effect on dreams. For example, in the fall in the northern parts of the United States, the leaves turn colors and then fall from the trees. This is a time of death and dying, the mysterious appears, and suddenly witches and spirits appear during Halloween.

When to Use Which Form of Dreamwork

Working on your dreams alone, by using sentient awareness and the breathwork method described in chapter 4, has both advantages and disadvantages over other methods. It is very deep, you can do it alone, and you're not necessarily dependent on anyone else. However, the disadvantage is that you must develop your lucidity and pick up sentient experiences of the Dreaming.

In the older, more analytical type of dreamwork methods, essentially you stand in consensus reality and think about the dream symbols. You try to interpret. You can play with those symbols, yet your reference frame remains consensus reality. However, there can be disadvantages to this kind of focus.

It stresses consensus reality and marginalizes the Dreaming. If analytical methods are the only methods used, they may cut the dreamer off from her own sentient process, which then makes the dream interpretation a theoretical speculation. In fact, such an interpretation might divert the dreamer from noticing the sentient processes and spontaneous energy happening in the moment.

Another problem with analytical dreamwork is that it tends to stress the wisdom of the analyst. Of course, most therapies do this. Without focus on the dreamer's momentary Dreaming, co-creativity is involved only incidentally, or only intellectually. Furthermore, many dreamworkers and dreamers run into relationship tangles when doing dreamwork because there are authority issues which are not being addressed that lie buried in the background of assumptions around whose wisdom is being used. This tangle occurs especially when people believe the interpreter is supposed to know more than the dreamer's own process, more than the Dreammaker.

Co-creativity is always present, to a lesser or greater extent, implicit or explicit, when working with another person. When co-creativity is present, working together with the parts of dreams and symbols is lots of fun and involves fantasizing together, storytelling, and having altered states of consciousness that I shall soon describe.

The advantages of co-creativity are the emphasis on entering into an altered state together and the democracy and equality of experience in mutual relationship. This mutuality may lead to artistic, unpredictable, even shamanistic experiences during dreamwork, since co-creativity is based on the life process inherent in the symbols. They are not just frozen images; they are more like twigs, which, when put back into water, sprout roots and can grow into trees. Like sprouts, symbols have the potential to grow.

In this chapter, I focus on the fluidity and creativity of symbols; in the next chapter my focus will be upon the *act* of co-creativity.

Symbols Cut from the Tree of Dreaming

In figure 13, dream symbols arise out of the Dreaming into Dreamland and then move further into the world of duality. Symbols are in the middle of my "tree of arising." As the Dreaming grows, it appears in dream images, as well as in movement, in sound, in feeling, in smell, in all the different sensory perceptual channels.

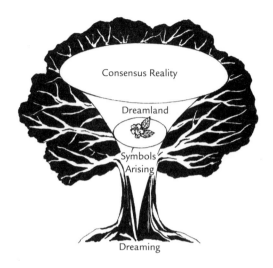

Figure 13. Tree of arising experience.

The basic idea is that the symbol is like a twig that you can cut off from a tree. The symbol that was cut out of the Dreaming from the night before will grow again if you put it back into the Dreaming, into the water, so to speak. A symbol is a twig, like this apple blossom cut from an apple tree (see figure 14).

Figure 14. Apple blossom on a twig from an apple tree.

If you stick that apple blossom twig in water, wait until it sprouts those fine silken shoots, and put it back in the ground. It will create another apple tree, just like the one it came from!

So symbols, although cut from the tree of Dreaming, are still potentially creative, even though they have been taken out of context, out of the Dreaming process. Put the symbol back into the water of Dreaming it came from, and you see the whole dream, not just the meaning or beauty of that particular symbol.

Why are symbols self-generating? That is a deep question and is probably connected to other difficult questions such as what is life, what is Dreaming, and how did the universe get created? How did the universe we live in come into being? How did it arise from the Big Bang and unfold into incredible diversity and the little planet called Earth?

I like the physicist John Wheeler's theory of how the universe works. Wheeler, who won a Nobel prize for his work on black holes, came up with a diagram of how the universe works and presented it at one of Albert Einstein's birthday parties. (See figure 15.)

Figure 15. Wheeler's diagram of the universe looking at itself.

Wheeler proposed that our universe is a fishlike being that gets curious about Itself and therefore looks back upon Itself. The universe began as a small being at the tail of the above diagram, "long ago," and Its mind is here "today" looking back in history. According to this model, ours is a self-reflective universe: It "thinks" about Itself. There is much in psychology and physics that supports this idea that the universe wants to know Itself. We need only think about the curiosity of children, and of our interest in new things. There is a primal tendency to notice things that "catch" our eye. We are always in a state of curiously looking at things.

The generalization of this tendency for us to look at things is that the universe is curious about Itself. This assumption of self-reflection is essential to understanding today's physics; it makes sense of quantum mechanics. (See my book *Quantum Mind* for more on this topic.)

You notice this self-reflection pattern in your dreams and in problems that are constantly repeating, reflecting themselves in everything you do, in your body, relationships, fantasies, and so on. The Dreammaker tends to be self-reflective; that is how It brings things to light: It generates Itself. Formulating this in mystical terms, I would suggest that the Dreaming creates duality as a way to look at Itself. It must be curious, creating endless parts and permutations and levels of reality that can reflect upon one another.

Let me suggest an experiment to you. Talk to someone about something that interests you, and tape it. Then write it up. You will see that you repeat yourself many times. The Dreammaker is inherently self-reflective. When It wants to get information across, It reflects and reflects upon Itself. The point is that, if you get into the Dreaming power of a symbol—if you get close to Dreamland—the symbol will grow further by itself and eventually explicate itself in terms that your everyday mind understands.

Talking about things that fascinate you, that occupy your mind, and that you are passionate about is a form of unfolding the Dreaming and its reflectivity. There are many ways of unfolding the Dreaming in this manner, such as what I call gossip and getting to the essence of symbols.

Gossip

Gossiping is a form of storytelling—usually an unconscious one—and it is one method of getting to the essence of a symbol, through unwitting amplification and reflection. Gossip includes saying amazing and forbidden things about someone, passing on information about another *something* that is not you. Gossiping and Dreaming are very close.

Usually, gossiping is looked down on. However, if you *consciously* gossip about a dream symbol, you give it lots of water, so to speak, so it can grow. Gossip with the dreamer in such a way that the dreamer forgets she's talking about the dream and loses herself in gossip about the part of the dream she is focusing on.

Say you dreamed about Aunt Molly. You tell me the dream and then we relax and start to chat. Suddenly, for no apparent reason you get interested in the roses in my room. You say, "Oh how wonderful your roses are over there." You go on and say, "Aunt Molly loves roses." I ask why she loves roses and you simply repeat that she loves them; in fact, her favorite activity is to grow them. You tell me that she feels best in her garden because she is like that garden, she is so "natural and sensitive."

When you've forgotten you were working on the dream, you have arrived at a slightly altered state called gossip or storytelling. Relax. Gossip is an incredible method of unfolding associations. They simply happen; they do not have to be "gotten." Information and associations arise spontaneously. The association to Aunt Molly is that she loves roses, and is natural and sensitive!

Gossip has a powerful advantage in getting to the meaning of symbols. It is spontaneous, not work. As long as you feel that you're "working" on the dream, you do injury to the Dreaming. The dreamer gets uptight. Instead of that, you need only let Dreaming do its own work. Gossip can help.

From Symbols to Dreaming

The most straightforward manner to get to the root of a symbol and let it dream further is to simply ask about that root. What is the tendency, the basic root of a symbol? What is the root from which the tree symbol has sprung?

For example, going back to Aunt Molly, you might ask the dreamer to remember Molly, describe her a bit, and then describe her essence, the Dreaming, the tendency that was there before it gave rise to Aunt Molly. The dreamer will have to ponder this for a while, and then sense that Aunt Molly and even the rose are just names for an almost nonverbalizable essence. In terms of words, the dreamer might say that the essence of Molly is like the rose, whose root is being exquisitely sensitive.

To get to the root of a symbol, you must describe it and ask about its essence—the sensation, the tendency the Dreaming—behind the symbol. Then you can enter into that essence, and It will unfold or reflect Itself until you experience Its meaning and what It wants to do in your life.

When working on dreams, let your ordinary consciousness relax so that you can immerse yourself in symbols, either through storytelling, gossip, or finding the Dreaming root. Dreaming will do the rest.

For example, let us say you dreamed about a special child. Instead of only interpreting that child as your spontaneity, you might ask yourself what is the essence, the root of that child, the energy that gave rise to that symbol of the child. There could be many answers to this question, but one might be happiness. Happiness might be the essence of a child in your dream.

Inner Work

To further train in gathering associations and finding their roots, try the following.

1. Choose a dreamfigure or symbol from one of your dreams. Describe that dreamfigure as exactly as possible.

2. Now try gossiping about that symbol. Say something forbidden or forgotten about that symbol. What stories and altered states—if any—appear while you are thinking or talking about that symbol?

3. Now feel your way into being a bit like that symbol, and explore its nature by asking yourself what power, energy, or essence gave rise to it. Find the Dreaming energy, the root of that symbol, and explore it. Feel it, be it, let it happen. Let it unfold. What does it become, or tend to become, in everyday life?

4. Finally, ask yourself why Dreaming used that symbol to express Itself.

 Things to Remember

1. Symbols are like twigs. Replant them in the Dreaming, give them water, and dreamwork happens as if by magic.

2. Gossip, tell stories, and gain direct access to the essence behind symbols to illuminate their meaning.

6

The Math of Dreams

I love to think in terms of mathematical metaphors, so please stay with me as I think mathematically about symbols. I know that as soon as I mention something about numbers, some readers grumble unhappily. Please relax; my use of math is more fun than what you may have been used to until now.

Recall that in chapter 5, I said a symbol is like a twig cut off from the main plant, the Dreaming. Given water, the twig sprouts roots and can be replanted to create new plants and flowers. Paradoxically, the twig is the outgrowth of a root, and at the same time, the twig can become the root of something new.

Symbols are like twigs. They came from the roots in the Dreaming, and as I shall show in this chapter, if replanted, symbols become the roots themselves for events in everyday life.

In chapter 5, you noticed how dreamlike images arise when you meditate on your breath. When you are in an altered state of consciousness, in a realm where the conscious mind is no longer the only manager of the situation, you notice how symbols appear as sentient experience arises and reflects upon Itself. With lucidity, you can track consciousness arising. As you track the arising of images in meditation, you notice how they not only arise out of that sentient emptiness, the Dreaming, but also unwittingly produce "your" ideas and actions in everyday life.

It is as if Dreaming produces an area for Itself in Dreamland, and the symbols of dreams in Dreamland produce their own areas in events of everyday life. Thus the root of everyday life is found in dreams, and the root of dreams can be experienced in Dreaming. Consider the example of Aunt Molly from the last chapter. Naturalness and sensitivity are the root of Molly as a dreamfigure, and she in turn may be the root of kind behavior in everyday life.

Mathematically speaking, if Dreaming, the root of all things, is symbolized by the letter X, then symbols that arise from this root and appear in Dreamland can be designated as X squared, or X times X. Mathematically, X squared can be written as X × X, or X^2. (Remember your math? The 3 squared is 3 × 3, or 9).

Mathematics says things in a nutshell. The root of X^2 is X, and X squared is X^2. When X, an experience in Dreaming, self-reflects, it squares itself. But what does squaring mean? When you take a line two inches long and square it, the line becomes a little square with an area of four square inches. Likewise, Dreaming, that is X, creates a space in Dreamland, or X^2. For example, if X represents a subtle and sentient experience such as sensitivity, then X^2 could be a dream symbol like Aunt Molly.

In any case, when Dreaming unfolds, It squares Itself into Dreamland. In the same manner, as symbols unfold in Dreamland, they square themselves, reflect upon themselves, creating an area in consensus reality, so to speak. In the example of the dream about Molly, sensitivity gives rise to Molly, and to kindness in everyday life. (If we wrote this out mathematically, it would be that $X × X = X^2$, and also that $X^2 \times X^2 = X^4$.) Dream events and symbols make room for themselves in your conscious mind. Although the Dreaming, dreams, and reality have different languages, they seem to unfold from one another along the same mathematical pattern.

As another example, remember the experience of Dreaming and the garbage truck I mentioned in earlier chapters. I was awakening and felt some disturbance. This is an "X." As I awakened further, this disturbance turned into symbols in Dreamland, the cymbals clashing in a symphony of some kind. These dream events are X^2. Finally, these musical, dreamlike events unfolded into everyday life and the garbage truck on the street. This final observation was an X^4, so to speak. The mathematical analogy shows us that the roots of what we call consensus reality can be found in dreams, and the roots of dreams are found in the Dreaming.

The basic idea is that processes of consciousness may be a kind of self-reflection like the squaring process. By analogy, finding the essence of an observation in everyday reality requires going back to its root.

All this means simply that the roots of everyday reality can be found in dream symbols, and the roots of symbols can be found in the sentient experiences of Dreaming. Let's use the following exercise to feel what all this means instead of thinking about it.

Inner Work on Squaring

Take a moment and notice what you are experiencing in the moment. When you are ready, explore the Dreaming going on in you right now by allowing your everyday mind to relax. Explore uncertainty and nonlocality by letting yourself be clouded and unknowing. Allow your mind to spread out beyond your body. Sense what is happening now that has not yet been formulated in your conscious mind. This may be irrational, and you may not yet understand the meaning of what is happening, but try to tolerate this state, and trust your Dreaming.

Now let that sense of what has not yet been formulated unfold. All you need to do is to track the unfolding. Tracking that sensation is like experiencing X unfolding into X squared. Follow some of those unknown sensations until they unfold into dream-like images. Good. Finally, let that image unfold further, or let yourself imagine what your life would have to be like if that image could have a space in your everyday life. Notice how you are thinking about how those images could live in everyday reality.

In any case, the mathematical formula for what you may have just experienced could be summed up as follows: Dreaming unfolds into Dreamland, which unfolds into everyday reality. Or, in formulaic terms:

Dreaming Unfolds into Dreamland,

$X \times X = X^2$

And Dreamland unfolds into Consensus Reality,

$X^2 \times X^2 = X^4$

That is the mathematical analogy of the way in which events arise out of the Dreaming into the awareness of everyday life. In terms of geometrical figures, this formula can be sketched out pictorially (see figure 16).

Practicing the Math of Dreamwork

The reason for all this fuss with mathematical analogies is that they can help us understand the practice of dreamwork. Dreaming unfolds into Dreamland and then into everyday reality. The problem that our dreamwork must address is that the remembered dream is only a glimpse of the experience of the Dreaming, and only part of the story from the domain of Dreamland. *To fully understand any one dream, you need to sense the Dreaming, the parts of Dreamland, and know about the dreamer's everyday reality.*

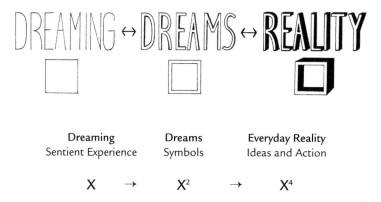

Dreaming	Dreams	Everyday Reality
Sentient Experience	Symbols	Ideas and Action

$$X \rightarrow X^2 \rightarrow X^4$$

Figure 16. A mathematical analogy of consciousness.

To appreciate a dream, you need to explore its essence, its source, and its roots in the realm of Dreaming. For example, the dream of cymbals clashing gives only limited sense of its Dreaming background. To know more about the cymbals and the world they are coming from, you must go back to their source in the Dreaming, to the archaic sense of disturbance. Likewise, to fully understand everyday reality, you need to find its roots in Dreamland. To understand the noise of that garbage truck, I have to know that I thought of it at first as a symphony! Only then will I be able to understand the parts and problems of everyday life and know that they may be all interconnected as if they were an unusual symphony.

At any one moment, in remembering any one dream, you get only bits and pieces of information about each world. Dreamwork sometimes reminds me of a game I used to play as a child, where you were given a few dots to put together. You had to connect them with your pencil to be able to see the figure that was hiding in the outline of those dots, so to speak.

Take a look at the incomplete information in figure 17. Notice the two vertical dashes above the title of "Dreaming" on the left. The image implicit in the two dashes could be a straight line. A box may be implicit in incomplete information in "Dreamland," and a large square in the incomplete information about "reality."

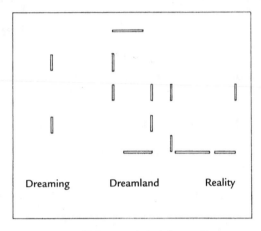

Figure 17. Incomplete information.

Gathering Information

The point is, in the beginning of working on a dream, we have only sketchy information, and we need to fill it in with more sensory-grounded experience, as well as information about the dreamer. We have already discussed different methods of gathering information about symbols via gossiping and gaining access to Dreaming. Now let's consider how to gather more information about the three domains shown in the sketch above.

To understand a dream, we need to collect, over time, in one way or another, the following information:

• The Dreaming or sentient experiences of the dreamer.

- The nature of the Dreamland symbol itself (through methods such as association).

- The details about interesting and problematic areas of the dreamer's everyday reality (through direct questions).

Gather More Information about Dreaming

To find out more about the general nature of the dreamer's Dreaming process, it may be helpful to notice or ask about the subtlest moods and feelings that can barely be verbalized. Pay attention to the dreamer's momentary body signals, for they are indications of the Dreaming; notice both comfortable and uncomfortable feelings. If you or the dreamer are not completely comfortable, ask for details about the vague discomfort. Dream symbols are related to these subtle moods and feelings.

Moods. Most of us do not talk readily about our moods; we have learned to marginalize them. But to understand the dreaming and interpret a dream, you must know what sort of moods move the dreamer during the day. (I will give an example below.)

Breathing and awareness. If the dreamer finds it difficult to connect with her moods and sentient experiences, ask her to focus on her breathing by counting on each exhalation from one to ten. Then, after the mind has been quieted, ask her to describe any subtle sensations and feelings. (This was described in chapter 4.)

Even with this preparation, some dreamers cannot say much about their most sentient Dreaming experiences. Don't force the situation. They don't have to focus on Dreaming; It is all around them. Since the Dreaming is nonlocal, you can feel the Dreaming:

Ask yourself about *your* sentient experiences while in the neighborhood of the dreamer. What is your deepest sense of being while you're with this other person? Unspoken feelings you are having when you are near the dreamer give you a sense of his or her nonlocal Dreaming. Do you feel dizzy, happy, sad, tired, hemmed in, or . . . ?

Sentient experience is nonlocal; that is, It knows no spatial boundaries. Therefore, you can explore how such experience applies to both you and the other person. Sentient experience connects you to the other. Pay attention either to your own or to the sentient experiences whenever possible.

Examples of Sentient Experience

When I asked one of my clients, Elisabeth, what sorts of feelings she had when she got up in the morning—feelings she normally marginalized or paid no attention to—she answered the following.

Elisabeth: Dreamy, very dreamy. I hate getting up!

I went further and asked if she had any recurrent problems that upset her in the morning or during the day.

Arny: Elisabeth, what sorts of feelings recur during the day that sometimes upset you?

At this point she could not answer, and for some reason, I began to feel uncomfortable, almost hasty, rushed. So I said to her that I felt rushed. To my great surprise, she responded as follows:

Elisabeth: Well, I feel sometimes rushed, from the outside. For some reason this reminds me of a dream in which my father was chasing me around the house! In reality I feel rushed.

In this example, Elisabeth's sentient experiences of dreaminess, hating to get up, and her, my, or rather our "nonlocal" rushed feelings, might be connected to specific dream characters—the one who is dreamy and the other who is chasing her about, the father.

Her mood and discomfort about getting up may be the sentient essence of the conflict between what appears in Dreamland as two parts of herself, the dreamer and the father who is chasing her (apparently to get things done in everyday reality). Let's not work further on the dream for the moment. I just wanted to give you a sense of how to collect information about the Dreaming and to see, in empirical terms, how the essence is nonlocal, and how it may "square" itself into various figures of Dreamland such as the father and daughter (see figure 18).

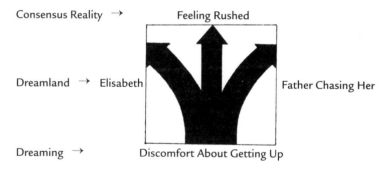

Consensus Reality →   Feeling Rushed

Dreamland → Elisabeth   Father Chasing Her

Dreaming →   Discomfort About Getting Up

Figure 18. Levels of Elisabeth's experience.

We have been exploring how to get information about Dreaming and about the connection between Dreaming and Dreamland. Now let's find out more about Dreamland. There are many ways to do this, some of which were mentioned in chapter 5. You can get to the sentient essence of symbols through meditating on them, by gossiping about them, by sensing them as twigs that produce roots, and also as the roots of events that grow from those twigs.

Associational Methods

Now let's begin exploring how to gather associations to the symbols that inhabit Dreamland. There are at least four kinds of associations:

1. Personal
2. Relational
3. Pop-up
4. Collective

The first type of association is personal. What do you, the dreamer, think or feel (or both) about a particular dream figure? That is, from your individual point of view, what do you think and feel about the other? This information is crucial to understanding why dream figures behave in dreams the way they do.

• The crucial question for the dreamer is, "What am I feeling or thinking about a particular dream figure?"

The second kind of association is relational. What does that other figure think about you, feel about you?

• The dreamer must ask herself, "What does that figure in my dream feel about me?"

Following Elisabeth's dream, for example, we would need to ask what her father thinks of her, what his feelings about her are.

In relational association, we ask, "What are the dream figure's associations to me?" It's important to know this for many reasons. For example, if you repeatedly dream of a critical person, and always seem to get negative feelings and interpretations about your dreams, you know that interpretation is coming from that dream figure and not from the larger, more deeply democratic part of you, the Dreaming. The inner critic always says you are a good-for-nothing terrible louse. That is definitely not the only possible interpretation.

The third kind of association is a "pop-up." It's like popcorn. What pops up in association to a given word? To get associations, you need an open, everyday mind. Getting the pop-up association is listening to the Big You, to the sentient world beneath a given dream image. You need to almost have a clouded mind, a relaxed experience where you are almost dreaming before you ask for a pop-up association.

• To get pop-ups, first create an atmosphere of relaxation and openness, of mindlessness, so to speak.

• Then ask yourself, "What pops up in association with the name Molly, or Father, for example?" You may need to say it a few times. *Molly . . . Molly. . . Molly.* Use different tones of voice; say the symbol-word with different feelings, and take the first words or experiences that arise.

Pop-ups are often surprising. The little you knows when you've gotten access to the Big You. It feels as if you have actually arrived in the Dreaming as more information starts to blossom forth, and there is no longer any need to *gather* information because it seems to be self-producing. A pop-up association, asked for in the right atmosphere, produces stories and storytelling; imagination simply begins to flow.

The fourth type of association is collective. C. G. Jung brought our attention to the collective or "archetypal" associations. What do different cultures associate with "Aunt"? What myths or fairy tales are there about aunts? What collective (whether ancient or modern) notions or sentiments are connected to a particular part of the dream? (For example, roses may be connected to love stories, Valentine's Day, etc.)

If you dream of a red car, an archetypal association might be "passion." Why? If you took a poll to find the consensual view of the color red, probably eighty percent of the population would say that red connotes strong feeling or passion. (By the way, someone recently told me the statistics for police stopping speeding cars. People with red cars get stopped the most. I was also told that they must pay a higher insurance rate too!) I have placed these four types of associations together in figure 19.

By combining all the associational, gossip-elicited, and collective information about symbols with their connections to dreaming roots, you will better understand your own and others' symbols. The dreamer will be thrilled with your joint work. To be complete in your work, you must know more about one more crucial domain: the dreamer's everyday consensus reality.

You need to gather information about the dreamer's everyday reality, its triumphs and travails, to assemble the most complete view of the dreamer. But before going on to this topic, gathering information about everyday reality, I want to illustrate how to use the information we have already gathered.

Another of Elisabeth's Dreams

A few weeks after our conversation and her recollection of the dream of her father chasing her, Elisabeth talked about how she felt so cozy one morning that, once again, she did not want to get out of bed. She remembered having had two dream fragments that night.

	1. Personal	2. Relational	3. Pop-Ups	4. Collective
What the dream symbol is	Dreamer's definition of symbol	What the figure thinks of you	Pops up, out of the blue	Collective information, stories, fairy tales
Interconnection between figures	Your relation to symbol	What the figure feels about you	The Big You's view of you and the other	General view of world and cultural history and the symbol's view of history
How to elicit the association	Talk about he figure	Ask what it thinks and feels about you	Create a clouded, open state of mind	Find and use general knowledge, and reference tools

Figure 19. Four types of associations.

In her first dream fragment she saw a lovely flower. In the second dream fragment she saw her "wonderful" friend, Nancy, who was "a very feeling person."

Those were her dream fragments, one about the flower, the other about the "feeling person," Nancy. We know a bit about her Dreaming; she said she felt "cozy." But we really don't know much about her Dreamland (or her everyday reality) yet.

I asked her for pop-up associations to flower, and she answered, "Flowers . . . hmmm . . . I just like them." She could not easily arrive at a pop-up; instead, she was telling me about her relationship to flowers: She "liked them." I took note of that and went on.

When I asked her for her pop-up association to Nancy, to her own great surprise she immediately said that "Nancy is like a flower, open and loving, and very present!" Her pop-up association was "loving, like a flower." Nancy is supportive to everyone. Elisabeth loves Nancy, who she says is also very playful. She then launched into all sorts of stories about Nancy's supportive nature.

She was so open to Nancy, I thought I would go further by asking what Nancy thinks about her, Elisabeth. She answered, "Nancy talks a lot about conflicts with her husband, who is always pushing her to work more, and she loves telling me those conflict stories!"

What Can We Learn from These Associations?

First of all, the two dream fragments about the flower and Nancy are connected: The symbols of *flower* and *Nancy* are synonymous ("Nancy is like a flower"). The relational association to Nancy helped fill in Dreamland. There is a flower, a loving, open person there, but also a "conflict" between Nancy and her husband: "Nancy talks a lot about conflicts with her husband, who is always pushing her to work more."

Recall the "chaser," represented in her earlier dreams by Elisabeth's father. The "chaser" is not represented directly in the present dream fragments about the flower and Nancy. Also recall that some weeks earlier, Elisabeth did not want to get up in the morning. She reported an ongoing tension between taking it easy, coziness, and working.

Without knowing more about her everyday reality at this point, we can already take a guess at a spiritual interpretation: From the viewpoint of Dreaming, Elisabeth is the hostess to the spirit of conflict between "cozy" feelings and the "push" of everyday reality. The psychological interpretation is centered on Elisabeth's identity and would be something like "Elisabeth is growing by getting to know parts of herself, her flower and its conflict with her pusher."

Figure 20 represents the unfolding events in Elisabeth's Dreamland and the Dreaming.

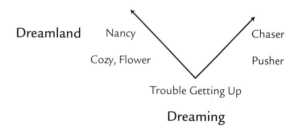

Figure 20. Elisabeth's dreams and Dreaming.

Information about Everyday Consensus Reality

From the viewpoint of consensus reality, both the spiritual and psychological interpretations are still a bit "up in the air" because they have not been related to Elisabeth's everyday life. So let's try to do that. To relate dreams to everyday reality, it is helpful to know something about the following areas:

- The dreamer's race and ethnic identity, sexual orientation, age, and religion.

- The particular nature of the dreamer's everyday relationships.

- The dreamer's health issues and body symptoms.

- The dreamer's economic class, work situation, however that is defined by her.

- The dreamer's community situation.

These questions may, of course, overlap. It takes hours to get a full picture of a person's various worlds; you may not be able to get all this information in one sitting. I am not suggesting that you do so. All this information is important, and needs to be collected in time, but not in a given moment.

Another central aspect of the dreamer's everyday reality is:

- What role does the dreamer play in everyday life?

By gathering information about the dreamer's everyday reality, you are getting to know the world the dreams are trying to take root in. Do you want to take a guess about Elisabeth's everyday reality? What do you think is her age, her work? What sort of reality were her dreams about her father chasing her and about her friend Nancy, unfolding into?

At the time of her dreams, Elisabeth was a Swiss client of mine in her forties, who came to me while I was working in Switzerland. Another one of my clients referred her to me. She was a "call girl," a "hooker" in downtown Zurich. During our first session she told me that she felt her work was meaningful, but she was frustrated. She had always wanted to be the head of an organization and had never done that. After the dreams about her father and Nancy, after Dreaming together with me in a way I shall describe in chapter 7, she decided to make a great change in her life. She wanted to go into the world and be more successful. After much thought, she opened her own call-girl business. Together with others, she made her relatively large, organized business, one of the first such legal entities accepted by the city. She became quite wealthy, and was thrilled to be of help to others. That was her way of putting the flower together with energy pushing her to create a new and expanded reality.

I realize that being a call girl may not be everyone's idea of success.[16] I had my own projections and prejudices to overcome about her work. Nevertheless, she managed to convince not only me but also the city of the human value of what and how she was doing things. Though she has let me mention her dreams, I prefer to not go further into the details of her work here. Perhaps it will suffice to say that her work suited her and she imbued it with her own integrity. She, too, was hosting the Dreammaker in her own way. Making a larger business out of her work and helping people was her way of being creative and happy and enjoying herself. She incorporated psychology into her work, and some of her "clients," whom she sent to me over the years, told me that she was not only successful but psychologically helpful as well.

The point of my story is this: The way in which Dreaming unfolds into everyday reality is unpredictable, creative, and almost always unexpected. Another point is mathematical: Dreaming

---

[16]In fact, as a dreamworker, it is best to be careful about the viewpoint from which you are interpreting dreams, and above all, don't forget the client's view.

squares Itself. Coziness unfolds into flowers and hastiness, which in turn unfold further into creating a new business and a fuller way of being in everyday reality.

 # Things to Remember

1. Dreaming is the (square) root of Dreamland, just as Dreamland is the (square) root of everyday reality.

2. To get a full picture of a person's Dreamland, elicit personal, relational, pop-up, and collective associations.

3. Explore the dreamer's roles in everyday reality, as well as issues around age, health, sexual orientation, race, religion, and economics.

7

Weaving and Altered States

We have been exploring how to gather information to fill in the incomplete sketch we have of Dreamland and everyday reality. We have considered how symbols are the square root of everyday reality and, twiglike, can grow roots almost by themselves. The next step is weaving; taking the threads of information you have about the Dreaming, Dreamland, and everyday reality and letting the Dreaming help in co-creating the story of life.

Dreamwork Is Group Facilitation

Most of the time, the little you tries to develop in a stepwise fashion. That is why the little you loves therapeutic prescriptions, advice, and dream interpretations that relate to mainly one part of the dream—"it means this, do that." However, if you maintain only that stance, after a while you may wonder, "If I have been developing one step at a time, why do I still have the same problems? Does this mean I haven't changed?"

One answer to this question is that the parts of the dreams may not change *unless your overall relationship to your Dreaming changes.* To change your overall attitude toward Dreaming, it is helpful to consider not only the psychological but also the spiritual interpretation of the dream, which views you as a hostess for manifesting the unfolding of dreams into everyday life.

While the psychological interpretation is oriented toward change and stepwise development, the spiritual interpretation is not. It says, there is nothing to change, nothing to do. *It* does things, *It* is happening; if anything, just notice, relate to the Dreammaker. Become aware that you are a hostess to your Guest. From the perspective of the Big You, the suffering of the little you is caused by not identifying with It, the Dreaming. If you identify more with the Dreaming realm, you do not feel judgmental or attached to the manifold worlds of dreams and everyday reality. Instead, you feel more willingness to "host" the unfolding, more open to your own altered states of consciousness and the viewpoints of the different figures in your dreams.

The closer you get to the Dreaming viewpoint, the more distance you have from any given part of yourself. You become like a group facilitator in your own dreams. The group of characters is your inner community; your dream parts are your group process. However, if you identify only with your waking self, you split your feelings off from the other parts and cannot facilitate your own inner world. Then you become dependent on someone else who is more deeply democratic, more open to your parts than you are.

In a way, learning to work on dreams is a way of learning to love. While the psychological growth involved in dreamwork is concerned with knowledge and understanding of parts, the spiritual key is learning to love. The closer you get to the Dreaming, the closer you are to becoming the Dreammaker's apprentice, a mystic lover, open to all parts of yourself and the world. The closer you get to the Dreaming, the less It must wait to manifest. In fact, as you draw closer, the less you feel that you have problems, and the more you have the sense of being part of an awesome experience instead.

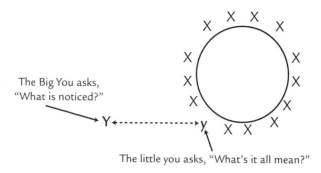

The Big You asks, "What is noticed?"

The little you asks, "What's it all mean?"

Figure 21. Dreamwork as group awareness.

Perhaps this is where mysticism, dreamwork, and social action intertwine. Although these dream and social-action worlds normally are considered separate, becoming a dreamworker requires the same development as a conflict facilitator, at least from the spiritual viewpoint. Both dreamwork and social action require access to the Dreaming, which is where the mystic lives.

In any case, the closer you come to the Dreaming, the more you become a facilitator, an open mind, a Buddha mind, someone who is free from what the Tibetan Buddhists call the "Wheel of Becoming." When you are *on* this wheel, you identify with everyday reality and are filled with problems, issues, worries, and the tug of opposites—shyness or power, politeness versus vengeance, peace verses conflict, life, or death. The questions you ask about dreams when you are *on* the Wheel are "What should I *do?*" or "What does this *mean?*" When you are *off* the Wheel, you accept these questions but also ask, "What do I notice?" In figure 21, notice the positions you (Y and y) have when you are both *on* and *off* the Wheel.

Dreamwork As Weaving

I can describe the nature and mathematical structure of dreams. However, catching and weaving the momentary power of Dreaming is an art that evades rational explanation. Weaving is co-creative.

After assembling information, you and the dreamer enter an altered state of consciousness and let the Dreaming weave a story. This part of dreamwork is more art than science. Nevertheless, a few pointers about weaving may be helpful.

The first step is to assemble all the information you have gathered from the various realms. These various pieces of information will be the "threads" to weave the final fabric:

• Sentient experiences occurring when awakening

• Pop-up associations to dream figures

• Personal associations to dream figures

• Collective associations to dream figures

• Relationship between the figures

• Sentient experiences behind dream figures

• Gossip about dream images

• Consensus reality identity, roles, age, health, economics problems, and so on.

The second step is to use the power of dreaming to weave.

Weaving relaxes your normal sense of identity and allows you to change momentarily as you enter the Dreaming. You remember the basic threads and notice how they come together on their own. Weaving is nonlinear. It is more like making music; you feel some sort of undefinable mood, hear a kind of tune or perhaps only a hum, and then begin to make music.

Likewise, in weaving you sense the Dreaming between you and

the dreamer and focus on the unspoken moods and feelings of both yourself and the other—while focusing mainly upon the dreamer. Weaving with the Dreaming is something that goes beyond all the information you have gathered; it is beyond the threads you will be weaving together. It is beyond words and comments, insights and understandings. You must listen closely to the facts and problems but also *feel the sound* of the Dreaming. When you really connect to the Dreaming, the dreamer will automatically join you in weaving. Then co-creativity happens on its own.

- Take the different threads and let the power of Dreaming weave them together.

  To begin with, in order to train your awareness of the weaving process, it might help to gather the threads and then choose a particular theme from the dreamer's everyday life situation. Perhaps you might even begin with an unsolved problem. Then sense the unspoken moods or feelings, and using these moods and feelings, begin to weave a story. Usually, choosing a heroine or hero of the story who is not the dreamer can be helpful.

  For example, if the dreamer is depressed, use that mood and begin very slowly and quietly: "Once upon a time, there was a person who lived in another city, at another time, who was not feeling very well because of the following problems. . . ."

- Note the use of nonlocal or open-ended times and spaces (locations) such as "once upon a time in another city, in another time," in a large hall or enchanted forest.

- Use an ally. While collecting information about the person's dreams and everyday reality, you will have noticed that certain dream figures or situations in Dreamland or everyday reality have been most helpful to the dreamer. If you remember them, use them now in the story, as special helpers or allies. If you were not told about such figures or situations, ask the dreamer if she has met certain special people or encountered meaningful events or activities that helped her to feel more comfortable, more fun and peace in everyday life.

For example, "In that faraway place and time, that person with those problems, who suffered so much, had a wonderful companion and ally who was at times fierce, loving, and wise."

- Note that the ally is the one who is most helpful and wise about Dreaming.

- Note that the ally gives comfort, support, or wisdom, or a combination of these.

For example, you might weave along with the other, saying, "That suffering person had an ally who had the most leisurely and detached sense of existence, a being who at times could become wise and fierce. . . ."And so forth.

Now it is time to let the dreamer co-create, and fill in the missing pieces and enter the state of storytelling.

Begin Weaving. Once the threads of the dreamer's existence, together with the dreamer's problem and the newly identified ally, have been established, go into an altered state of the moment. Don't try to *think* the story through. Just notice the Dreaming, the unspoken mood happening in this very moment. Don't fight that mood or try to change it—*use it as a vehicle*. Go into that unspoken mood and discover its particular coordinates—its space and time, its world, so to speak. Then "step into" the altered state of consciousness, into the world that mood creates, and know that you are in the Dreaming.

For example, one client I worked with said that he had been

wrestling all day long with undefinable energies. He told me about his woes in a mood of confusion and bewilderment. What should he do? I felt bewildered as well, and began to use that mood to weave with. I used that confused state and said in the most bewildered mood I could produce, "Once there was a man who was so confused he did not know what to do."

Instantly my dreamer-client joined me and said, "Yes, and this man bumped into a special person called Harry the Hippie who was in such an altered state of consciousness that he was dreaming all day long." At this point my client stopped co-creating with me and burst out laughing so hard, tears came to his eyes. "I am too square," he said about himself, "too normal, too straight and boring! I forget to relax and enjoy life, to take this existence as an awesome trip."

The point here is that in weaving you begin by feeling, sensing, and moving with the momentary Dreaming, creating a story. Use the space and time and power of the dreamer's unspoken mood to tell the story. Don't work at it. Let the story be dreamed up by the situation. If the person is happy, climb into happiness and let that carry you. If the dreamer sounds depressed, explore misery and slow rhythms in telling the story. To do this, you need to relax your everyday mind; do not try to be therapeutic or helpful, but focus on your—or rather "Its"—creativity instead.

Enjoy the energy of creativity; be shamanistic in your story-telling. Use your hands; touch the dreamer's body (in a place that feels appropriate to the dreamer, such as the hand or arm) as you talk to him or her. (If you have not had bodywork training or are uncomfortable touching the person, just use your voice.) Tell the story as if it were the greatest, most fabulous story ever told. Transform yourself into the power of the dreamer's Big You, detach from success and failure, and be one of the spirits creating life.

The Big You is a natural weaver; It loves repeating things and bringing things together, It loves stories and fantasies. In working with dreams, the most challenging personal job is to learn how to let go of the familiar little you and all its attachments to limitations and judgments and open to this Big Mind, the Big You that is boundless.

As you tell the story, you probably will not have to explicitly invite the dreamer to take part in the co-creation of the story, although occasionally some dreamers do need a verbal invitation. If the dreamer is shy about doing this, invite the dreamer to imagine being a child with you, for the child is that uninhibited dreamer in all of us.

In any case, at this point, both of you are now in an altered state; you are in a sort of musical duet and you can sense again what creativity and art are all about. It is something to enjoy and allow to occur.

Retelling the Story. Once the story has been created, don't assume that the work of co-creativity is done. Repetition may still be needed for the conscious mind to get the point. Retell the story.

For example, in the case of my bewildered client and the story of Harry the Hippie, before we parted I had to retell just how Harry the Hippie loved love, and thought it was a great "trip." Each time I told the story, my client burst out with laughter, and each time, the significance of the story seemed to deepen.

Retelling is a crucial part of the work. Repeat the story; it reflects the Dreaming and sends the dreamer a particular message. The retelling of the story is, itself, another co-creative act.

Retell the story and bring in the nature of Dreaming: democracy. Try to remain democratic, seeing each part of the story as equally significant. You can train in storytelling by asking questions, by gathering information, and by making stories all day long about everything, anything, and anybody. Feeling excitement and amazement about something is a precious gift from the Dreaming that wants to be unfolded and shown in all of Its magnificent facets and parts. From the viewpoint of Dreaming, creativity is what life is all about. Give birth to the stories gestating in the Dreaming.

A Dream That Switzerland Was a Small Country

Another story comes to mind from one of my Swiss clients. I will go into detail in retelling her situation, to give you an idea about how weaving might proceed.

Dream. She dreamed that someone announced on the radio that Switzerland was a small country and that it took only four hours to travel through it by car from one end to another.

Everyday Reality. In her everyday life, she was a teacher at a Swiss university. Her basic problem was wondering what she should be doing with her life: Was she meant only to be a teacher? Should she stay in Switzerland?

Gathering Information. I asked her about relational associations: What did Switzerland think about her? She told me that she felt as if Switzerland did not like her because she was very unconservative in the way she dressed and spoke out in public. She told me that Switzerland was a little country and could not tolerate her because she did not easily follow its rules. Being small, Switzerland had to be strict, to protect itself, but she did not like its strict nature.

Allies. When I asked her if she had any allies—any friends or events that gave her a sense of well-being and peacefulness or brought her encouragement and wisdom—she said that whenever she needed help, she would simply sleep. *Sleep* was her ally. She said she could often relax, fall asleep, and find answers to her questions during those in-between moments of awakening.

The Dreaming. At the time she told me this dream, she seemed unhappy, sluggish, even bored. When I began to process the dream with her, I decided to use that sluggishness as a vehicle to travel with, so to speak. I stepped quietly into a sort of sluggish, easygoing rhythm, an almost bored state of consciousness. I even began to feel a bit unhappy as I began storytelling. I recalled some of the "threads" of information she had told me about, and spoke as if doom were upon us:

"Once upon a time, many years ago before there were many roads in her section of the world, a teacher wandered slowly over the landscape until she found a town where she thought she might work. She was feeling ill. The clouds above were very dark; she had almost no energy and felt she was barely able to do anything, much less teach in that town, work at her job of teaching. In fact, to her own surprise, she wondered if she was meant to be a teacher at all."

I noticed that at this point the dreamer felt "spoken to" because she asked how I knew all this about her. Without answering, I motioned that she should join me in the tale, but she preferred to remain in a listening mode instead. I continued.

"One day, while she was walking through town, someone asked her where she came from. She said she was from Switzerland, a small country far away, with high mountains."

At this point, the dreamer immediately entered the story, saying, "Yes, that Swiss country was indeed very, very little, very special, and to survive, it developed its own peculiar nature. People there became very inward, and they lived in caves!"

We both started to laugh, and the mood changed. I proceeded, saying in a mysterious voice that the townspeople were amazed to hear about this amazing country of Switzerland from where the wandering teacher had come. My client went further, proclaiming suddenly, "The teacher was happy to have left Switzerland, and did not know whether or not she should ever return."

I tried to bring her ally into the story. "Listening to her, sitting in front of a little shop on the main street of that little town, was a very old and sleepy woman who said magical things. She looked as if she was almost asleep when she spoke, saying—"

In a sort of groggy voice, my client piped in at this point, "That old sleepy person suddenly spoke, mumbling . . . mumbling . . . stay in Switzerland while you're out in the world. Stay inside while outside!"

As soon as my client spoke those words, she stopped telling the story and enthusiastically proclaimed that her task was not just to teach, to leave or stay in Switzerland, but rather, to *stay deep within herself while she was teaching*. Not the place or the content of what she taught was the important thing, but *the manner in which she did things*. She decided she would be "Swiss!" This meant for her to be quiet, introverted—and be "a small country" even while she was teaching, doing things in the world.

She no longer looked depressed, but centered and peaceful. I repeated her story about the teacher who came to town and heard the mumbling of a sleepy old woman who said that she should stay inside while outside in the world. While speaking, I gently touched the top of her forehead for some reason. She told me that she often had pain in her head, headaches, when teaching, and had been thinking about quitting that profession. Now she felt better, especially when she listened to the retelling of this story. It related to her inner and outer experiences, and incorporated her ally—her sleep—that often came up with answers. Apparently her headaches were linked to her conflict between her inwardness and her relating to other people.

If you give It a chance, you will notice that Dreaming is full of stories and solutions, just ready to pop out. Perhaps the following exercise will help you experience the "story-readiness" inherent in Dreaming.

Co-creative Dreamwork

This exercise is described so that you can do it with someone else, or with yourself. Take a moment, and . . .

Recall a Short Dream.

Gather Information About Dreaming, Dreams, and Everyday Reality.

1. Note the momentary dreaming experience. Notice any moods, frustrations, sensations, and feelings.

2. Find out about Dreamland.
   • Ask about the personal, relational, and pop-up associations to the main symbols.

Embellish with collective meanings.

Don't forget to gossip about the images!

3. Find out about everyday reality.
   • Note problems and details about issues related to, age, health, relationships, work, family, community, time, location, economics, race, religion, gender, sexual orientation, etc.
   • Note identity and roles played in world.

4. Find an "ally"—an event, dream figure, person, or feeling—from daytime or nighttime experiences that evoked a sense of inner peace or centeredness. Then take a moment and imagine the world it lives in, that is, the sense it must have of time and its sense of space. Feel that time and space, and explore what it is like to live there.

Co-creativity: Weaving the Threads of Dreamwork

1. Notice the Dreaming, the unspoken mood happening in this very moment. Don't fight it: use it as a vehicle, an altered state of consciousness from which to begin creating a story in another time and space. Notice, describe, and repeat that Dreaming.

   Take as the main theme of the story the person's problems and life identity. At some point in the story, bring in the helpful ally.

Let the threads of the story (the gathered information) weave themselves, and encourage the dreamer to join you in weaving the tale. Remember to remain attuned to the mood of the present Dreaming, letting it reveal different things.

You might begin the story:

> *Once upon a time, not too long ago and in a faraway place, there was a woman [or man] with . . . problems related to her age, her health . . . her gender . . . her economic situation and her job. . . . Other people also troubled her in the world, namely . . .*
>
> *Nearby were dreamlike figures and events [take these from the dream]. Some of these figures added to her well-being, others confused her about life.*
>
> *Happily, a helpful ally figure spoke to that woman [or man] about her problems, saying . . .*
>
> *After this message, our dreamer began to change in an uncanny and unpredictable manner. She was no longer . . . but rather. . . . She no longer identified with her little self or unconsciously identified with others, but rather grew in the following way. . . . She saw herself suddenly solving the problems of her everyday life using the world of, and information from that ally. She realized . . .*

2. Finally, retell the dream and explore its implications. When the mood is near ordinary awareness again, talk about the everyday realities of the dreamer and comment on how this story is connected to the sentient feelings of the dreamer, her comfort, frustrations, and happiness. Ask her to make a note of her insights.

3. Interpret the dream. Practice being helpful by remembering how the dreamer's awareness might expand to include the ally and the Dreaming. Ask the dreamer what changes in everyday life might

occur because of the Dreaming. Then describe the dreamer as a hostess to that story, a person who is being asked to manifest the essence and truth of that story in everyday life. Make a note about being such a hostess.

Whose Dream Was It?

When you are done, it will probably occur to you that you and the dreamer share a similar personal development. From the viewpoint of everyday reality, the story you created together is not just the dreamer's; it is yours, too. In this sense, you and the dreamer now have a shared development. This is one of the exciting aspects of working with someone else on her or his dream. You change because the Dreaming connects everything, because of the story; you too are a hostess for that story. The work you did "for the dreamer" is yours as well. You are always self-healing, even if it looks as if you are facilitating someone else's healing.

From the viewpoint of Dreaming, there is only one client and one dreamer: your whole self, You. If you identify with the Dreaming, with the Dreammaker, the Big You, if you identify with creative intelligence behind life, the spiritual interpretation of the dream is clear: "It" is creating, presenting the little you and me with enlightenment, conflict, trouble, and pain. "It" is the perennial Guest. It knocks on your door, It knocks on everyone's door—and says, "Please let me in." Sometimes it seems to me that God is knocking, asking to be let in. Asking someone to be Its apprentice.

Today most education systems and cultural milieus do not encourage us to notice the Dreaming. Too few of us have learned to open our doors when It knocks. The little you behind the door is much too busy with everyday reality. The little me has no time; the little you is too attached to being depressed or elated, happy or unhappy. Nevertheless, regardless of the openness of the little you, the Guest knocks, and enters whenever It wants to. As long as we marginalize the Dreaming, we fear that Guest, our own unpredictable, creative, and unfathomable nature.

The principles of Dreaming involving mathematical squares and square roots, symbols and twigs, Dreamland and consensus reality help us in understanding the unpredictable nature of life. However, without the storytelling process itself, these principles are unable to portray the magical nature of weaving and co-creative dreamwork.

Things to Remember

1. The information you have gathered, together with unspoken moods and feelings, become the vehicle and the path, carrying you into and out of storytime.

2. Open the door and let in the Guest.

3

DREAMING WITH FLIRTS
How to Interpret Dreams with Flirts!

8

Fast Cats Catch Flirts

In part 1, we focused your awareness on the subtle experiences arising in connection with breathing in order to notice the Dreaming and to interpret your dreams. In part 2, we explored the creative power of symbols and Dreaming, how Dreaming "replants" symbols as if they were twigs, so to speak—and how to use the deepest moods of the dreamer to co-create stories.

In part 3, we will explore how flitting, evanescent, flashlike perceptions can be used to access the Dreaming and more fully understand your dreams. I call these perceptions "flash-flirts."

What Is a Flash-Flirt?

Perceptions come in many sizes, shapes, and kinds. Some last long enough to be easily identified and spoken about; others last only a split second—the "flash-flirts." I speak of them as flashes because they happen in the blink of an eye, like a lightbulb that flickers on and off "in a flash." My usage of flash is meant to convey the evanescent nature of flickering perceptions. A flash-flirt is a flickering, short-lived, transient sighting (see figure 22).

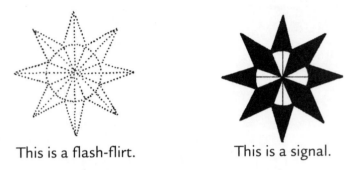

This is a flash-flirt.　　　　This is a signal.

Figure 22. The difference between flash-flirts and signals.

I use the notion of a *flirt* to convey how the flash "tempts" you; it is as if it tries to catch your attention. In contrast, a signal is strong enough or long-lasting enough to be recognized and easily shared with others.[17] For example, an Aboriginal Australian living in her native setting might experience a tree as having the power to catch her attention, as "flirting" with her, so that she is drawn to look at the tree. The tree sort of winks at you, and then, because of that flirt, you find yourself drawn to look at it. In Aboriginal thinking, objects have power to catch our attention by (my word) flirting with us before we look at them.

We find the basic idea of these flash-flirts not only in Aboriginal thinking, but also in physics. One way of understanding the process of

---

[17]You can find a longer introduction to flash-flirts in my study of quantum phenomena and in-depth discussion about similar concepts found among Aboriginal Australians; see chapters 15 to 18 in *Quantum Mind: The Edge Between Physics and Psychology*. Also see chapters 3 and 4 in *Dreaming While Awake, Techniques for 24-Hour Lucid Dreaming*.

observation in quantum theory is to consider particles as entities that "flirt" with you in virtual reality before you actually see and observe them as signals.[18] The flirting back and forth in virtual space between you and the object, or between any observer and the thing to be observed, is a virtual reflection that we might experience as a *flirt,* and which quantum physics imagines within the context of the mathematics of physics.

Flash-flirts (under other names) appear as well in the Buddhist text the *Abhidhamma,* the text of higher learning where reference is made to "evanescent" feelings, thoughts, and sensations that quickly arise and pass.[19]

Seen within the context of the levels of awareness—the experience of Dreaming, Dreamland, and everyday consensus reality, flash-flirts occur somewhere between the Dreaming and Dreamland. Flirts are one of the first indications of the Dreaming that the conscious mind can perceive, and occur so quickly, you tend to forget them. One moment something is there, then it is gone. To demonstrate flash-flirts in one of my classes, I turned my back on the class, wrote the word "nose" on a piece of white tape, and stuck it to my nose.

Then I whipped around to face the class and just as quickly turned my back again and took the tape off. Facing the class again, I asked them what they saw.

One person said, "I saw a sticker with nothing on it."

Another said, "It said 'wise'!"

Another said, "I saw a Band-Aid."

---

[18]I am thinking here in particular of the work of physicist John Cramer from the University of Seattle, whose work on explaining the quantum wave reflection system in terms of electronic machines was meant at first to be nothing more than an analogy. For more on this see my *Quantum Mind,* chapter 18.

[19]See chapter 4 of my *Dreaming While Awake, Techniques for 24-Hour Lucid Dreaming.*

Figure 23. The nose.

Still another said, "It said 'noisy.'"

Someone said, "No, the last letter was E."

I explained that the content of the message on my nose was simply "nose." I wanted to show the following two points in this experiment:

Consensus Reality Uncertainty. Because of the speed of the flash-flirt, you become uncertain about the content. You know something happened, but you don't know what.

Difference between Consensus Reality and Dreamland Experience. The consensus reality content of the message—namely, the tape with the word "nose" written on it—is a very different experience than the Dreamland experience of the piece of tape. In Dreamland, that tape was experienced as saying *nothing, wise, Band-Aids,* and *noise.* These expressions are the way in which the Dreaming used the personal dictionaries of individuals to express Itself through associational processes. Though we get a personal message from flash-flirts, all we can know for certain is that some form of energy or power manifested itself.

118

Using Flash-Flirts

In these next chapters, I will be using flash-flirts to explore the meaning of dreams. By definition, flash-flirts are evanescent; that is, they occur so rapidly, you tend to marginalize them and not take them seriously because you are uncertain about their exact message and meaning.

Nevertheless, the body registers the flirts through sudden breaths, eye and eyebrow micromovements, and slight vocalizations. When you have seen a flirt, you might take a sudden slight breath, or your eyebrows and eyes might move very rapidly in a quick gesture of surprise. Sometimes you might make a slight sound at the same time, like *ha,* or *oh.* You will probably forget what made you take that breath or move that eyebrow unless you have trained your awareness, are quick, and ask yourself, "What flirted with me?"

One of the disadvantages of working with such quickly passing flirts is that the work requires lucidity, quick awareness on the part of the dreamer. You need to be really quick and lucid to catch these things, and you have to be in a special, lucid state of mind. You have to be quick as a cat, looking for a mouse.

Most therapists and dreamworkers are not in such a lucid or "fast cat" state of mind; they are more like a "gentle cat," lying about in a more ordinary state of mind, looking for information, for content, in contrast to focusing on evanescent processes. Looking for personal history and associations is very different from being aware of quickly passing perceptions.

If you are going to be an ordinary dreamworker, you can be a gentle cat. However, if you want to work with flirts, there is no way around it, you must become a fast cat.

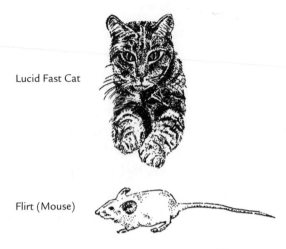

Lucid Fast Cat

Flirt (Mouse)

Figure 24. Flirting mouse and lucid fast cat.

Figure 25. Gentle cat, observer of signals and content.

Your Work Depends on Your Training and Your States of Mind

If you've been trained to look for movement, you will see movement. If you've been trained to look for dream symbols, you'll see archetypes. If you've been trained to notice which directions the eyes move in, you will see that. If you are trained to act things out, you will look for scenarios to role-play. Your training and state of mind determine the information you gather.

Most of the states of mind I have mentioned so far are involved in focusing on information, content, learning, education, parts, and the "little you." Each mind-set—including that of fast cat—has limitations. One of the limitations of the mind-set of the "Big You" that looks for quick things as well as overall pictures is that you pay attention to things that seem worthless to everyone else. You look for ignored perceptions, flash-flirts, and you address spiritual and sentient dimensions of reality that others tend to marginalize. Each mind-set thinks it is better than the others are. However, there is no doubt in my mind that we need them all, at one time or another, to work on dreams.

How Flirts Help You with Dreams

Let me give you an example of how a flash-flirt can help to explain a dream. Consider a weekend situation in which Amy and I are working in our Portland apartment. We are catching up on business, making calls, dealing with emergencies, trying to find time to go jogging, and so forth. However, people keep disturbing us, ringing our front doorbell. Outside on the street below, a car alarm goes off. Those alarms seem to go off frequently in our neighborhood for some reason! *Deedoo, deedoo, deedoo.* As I sit at my desk in our apartment, I find myself saying, "Oh, that damn car alarm!" Then I forget that alarm as soon as I have noticed it.

I barely recall the alarm, that flash-flirt, even though it was right there in my awareness a moment before. I was in the mind-set of a busy or gentle cat, but not a fast cat. The alarm was an incomplete signal, like a sentence that is begun but not completed. You cannot grasp its meaning, so you forget it. I almost forgot that car alarm.

Then my "fast cat" awareness awoke. I realized, oh, I was marginalizing that alarm. The thing that was filling my mind was the business on my desk and the disturbances I was experiencing that morning. There we were in the midst of the city, people knocking on the door, the telephone constantly ringing and so forth. Being therapists, we sometimes have people coming to the door asking for help. Sometimes there just seems to be too much to do; I was getting irritated with the front door.

Then I recalled the alarm: *deedoo, deedoo*. I focused on it, and its message was something like "—Breaking in!—Stop!"

That was the overt content of the flirting alarm. The Dreaming, the sentient essence behind it, was very different. I asked myself what energy was there before the alarm even sounded. As I felt into that space, I realized that the Dreaming behind the flirt was an exquisite sensitivity that, when disturbed, naturally reacts—and if this is not heard, the sensitivity reacts loudly, indignantly.

I felt my way into the state of that Dreaming, the state of that sensitivity behind the flash-flirt—not the alarm itself, but the sensitivity at its essence. This gave me the experience of being very centered and sensitive. This experience changed my mind-set, and instead of just seeing things from the viewpoint of consensus reality, as I had been doing, I now had a new and more detached perspective.

From this centered and sensitive state, from the viewpoint of the Dreaming, I could see the value of little Arny doing his work. From the same viewpoint, I could also see the value of those people at the door that Arny called disturbances. Without those disturbances, Arny could never really know Me, the Dreaming, this sensitivity. From the viewpoint of the Dreaming, both Arny and "the disturbers" are Me. I created them both. As long as I was looking at the situation from the viewpoint of the Big Me, the Dreammaker, I understood the value of those disturbers and the little Arny's viewpoint.

In any case, after a few minutes, the next caller came by, banging on our front door. When I got to the door, I surprised myself. I was actually happy to see that person, thanked him for coming, and then, to my own surprise, burst out crying like a baby because there were too many disturbances. The invader, whom I had never met before, was shocked to see me cry. That person said he had learned something and went away, looking amazed. Actually, both of us were shocked and amazed. In the Dreaming, I knew that that person must have been another me who needed to learn how to cry when things get to be too much. Moreover, at the same time, in the midst of all that, it was awesome to have been detached, sensitive, and crying, all at once.

Finally, I thought about the dream I had had the night before. I dreamed I saw trees that grew next to one another so that they made a diamond shape in the forest (see figure 26).

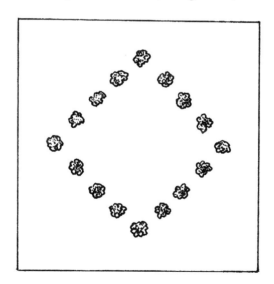

Figure 26. The trees formed a diamond shape.

What did I associate with the diamond? The first associations that popped up were *eternity* and *invulnerability* because diamonds do not scratch easily; they are extremely hard and invulnerable. And with trees, I associated their amazing sensitivity. The pop-up association with trees brought me even more information. The pop-up brought me back an old memory of a time when I was a child. I used to sit in a tree in front of my family home and spontaneously interact with visitors from the branches above the ground. While sitting in that tree, I could hide and not be seen by visitors, and behave freely, like a proverbial little trickster, dropping down on their heads tiny things to make them realize that I was sitting in a tree!

That pop-up made me laugh. It helped me understand my dream. I needed those trees and that freedom and detachment to play and interact with the visitors, as I had done when I was a child, sitting in the tree. The flash-flirts and the Dreaming had brought back my tree position from which I could freely deal with visitors by letting all my reactions out. The Dreaming had brought me to a sensitive place (the trees), which had the highest psychological value symbolized in the dream by the diamond formation of the trees. Being a fast cat with that alarm had enabled me to get to its sentient essence of sensitivity.

Now the dream was clear. Trees are valuable diamonds! As long as I was not in contact with my inner trees—with that sensitive vegetation in myself—disturbances only upset me. Becoming more sensitive and fluid, being free to behave as I felt, was a form of self-protection making me feel both more sensitive and, paradoxically, less vulnerable to the outer situation.

The moral of the story is that the sentient essence (in this case, sensitivity) of a flash-flirt (like a car alarm) is the Dreaming behind dreams and everyday life. *The sentient essence of flirts is the root of dreams.*

The following exercise is meant to help you explore flirts and their relationship to your dreams. Again, having a pencil and paper near at hand, will be helpful.

The Big You and Flash-Flirt Exercise

1. Recall a dream you had recently; any dream or dream fragment will do. Choose a particular part of it you would like to explore the most. Make a note of it now.

2. Now take a moment or two and try to relax; take a couple of deep breaths, and slowly allow your eyes to close for a moment. When your eyes feel ready, let them open slowly. Slowly gaze around where you are sitting, standing, or lying. Although you are relaxed as a whole, use your "fast cat" attention and catch the first object, person, color, design, or material that your attention focuses on. If several things catch your attention, let your unconscious mind choose which object or event to focus on. If you are blind, you can use the first sound or feeling that catches your attention.

3. Now take a moment, and hold that object in your attention; keep your focus on that object. Hold it as closely as you can. When you are ready, feel your way into it. Try to imagine that you are within that object, in fact, that you are the object. Use your hands or facial expression or sitting posture to make some sort of motion that expresses the object's nature, or make a sound that it might make. Don't be shy about movement; make a hand motion that expresses the nature of the thing that has caught your attention. Even make that hand motion again. Now make a note about that object and motion.

4. Now decrease the motion, the sound. In fact, make no motion or sound at all, but instead, simply *feel* the energy that is behind the

thing that caught your attention. Get to the root, the seed, and the essence of the object, an essence that was there before it became an object, so to speak. This root may be only a slight sensation at first. Nevertheless, it is important.

Take a moment and try to get to the essence of that sensation, its root. This is how to get to the Dreaming essence behind the thing that caught your attention. Stay with the essence right there. Be there. Be that Dreaming. Stay in that state. Don't be hesitant. Let that state be, and give yourself a chance to experience it. Just be there in the experience of the essence of the thing that caught your attention.

5. Be in the essence of the world of Dreaming. Now you are close to the Dreaming. This is an eternal aspect of yourself, the Big You, the state of oneness and creativity that gives rise to all other things. Be in that state and allow yourself to feel and imagine how life might be if you were close to this essence. Take your time with this essence. Make a note of the energy of the essence.

6. Finally, reconsider the dream or part of a dream you recalled in step one. Do you have associations with that part of the dream, that figure or figures? Make notes of those associations now. How is this dream, or part of the dream, connected to your experience of the essence that occurred in step five? Try describing the figures and actions of that dream in terms of their relationship to the energy of the world of Dreaming. Are they reactions to it, or representations of it? Explore what these figures might represent.

The Dreaming state of mind that came from working with flirts helps to arrive at a deep understanding of the dream, its source, and the essential reason for the dream. This is a nondualistic understanding; it does not evaluate things in terms of good and bad. Things are simply *there;* they are all needed to express the Dreaming.

Advantages of Flash-Flirts

An advantage of working with flirts is that they are always present; they are the living Dreaming. People don't always dream, but these sudden perceptions are always occurring.

An interesting moment happens when both you and the dreamer see the same flirt at the same time, such as a sound, or a passing bird. Then it's clear that you're Dreaming together. That shared experience bonds the two of you, and you can work on the flirt together as if you both have the same psychology.

Of course, anything that I notice about your perception is, in principle, a perception of mine. We are both seeing it. So, in a way, dreamer and dream interpreter are *always* Dreaming together. The *essence* of what we perceive may be the same, though its manifestation is experienced differently by each of us.

To know yourself and the other dreamer, wait and watch. Be a fast cat and notice the things that flirt with her or him. Then try going to the essence of these things yourself, and inviting the dreamer to do so as well. That's the best way of finding the Dreaming, the power that is using both of you to express Itself. Working with flirts is shamanistic. Flirts are the closest thing you can get to having your own guru sitting right there in front of you, because flirts inform you about Yourself in highly wise and learned ways—if *you* learn how to wait and watch and notice.

The Barbell

I recall a playful example of working on a dream with an eight-year-old client who was sent to me because he had a severe case of asthma. The little boy, surrounded by his parents, told me in a fear-ful voice that he dreamed of a big tractor crushing a house. His mother and father were nervous because they thought this dream might mean he could be crushed by his asthma. "After all," they explained, "his asthma attacks almost killed him once, sending him to the hospital emergency ward."

When I began to work with the little boy, I asked him what he asso-ciated with that tractor, "What do you think about tractors?" The child immediately said, "Tractors are very, very big and can change anything!" At this point his parents chimed in, saying that he was a tractor, crash-ing everything they owned. He tends to be "hyperactive," they said.

Instead of going further with their comment or dream itself, I began to chat with him and his parents about his health. They wanted me to notice that the child was wheezing in the moment; the child's breathing was troubled by asthma. While I was saying something to his mother, I saw the child's attention briefly go to one of the little five-pound barbells in my office. The child's attention quickly came back to what I was speaking about with the parents.

I noticed the "flirt"—the barbell—and suggested that he and I focus on the barbell. When I asked the child to lift that barbell, the father said it would be too heavy for him. "Oh no," the child insisted, "I can do it, I am big and strong," and immediately went to the barbell to lift it and with some effort, succeeded.

I applauded, and then asked the child to pretend he was a barbell. The little boy had no trouble with that and said he was "all iron, big and strong." Then he said spontaneously, "Just like that tractor in my dream." I suggested just feeling the power of being heavy and ironlike might be fun too, and the child sat quietly, puffed out his chest a bit, and became "heavy iron." The breathing symptoms of his asthma disappeared.

In this case, the energy of the flirt, that is the barbell, helped with understanding not only the dream, but the body symptom as well. The child needed to have more conscious access to his own sense of powerfulness even when he was quiet. At this point, outside my office, a huge tractor making lots of noise moved by on the street. We all laughed and laughed!

Where Flirts Fit into the General Scheme of Things

In the earlier chapters, I mentioned how there is no "I"—no primary identity or ego state associated with the realm of Dreaming. As we know from the previous exercise, flirtlike events just happen. In contrast to the energy of Dreaming, which produces those flirts, the events of Dreamland usually have more differentiable parts, figures, and events. There is no consensus on their existence because each person's Dreamland is unique to him or her.

Flirts occur somewhere in between Dreaming and Dreamland, in between the states of nonduality and dualism. There's no "I" associated with a flirt; they go underneath and around, and beyond what the little you focuses on. Yet they are experienced at first as something that is not-me.

When a flirt persists and becomes a differentiable signal that you remember and begin to think about, it has become a figure in Dreamland waiting to unfold into everyday reality. See the position of flirts in the spectrum of awareness in figure 27.

Flirts and Synchronicity

When you are in a normal state of consciousness and events occur in the outer world (the tractor on the street) that reflect inner experiences (the child's sense of being a tractor), C. G. Jung said, a "synchronicity" has occurred. Likewise, when inner experiences mirror the outer world, synchronicities are said to have occurred. Jung defined synchronicity as a coincidence of meaning, a situation

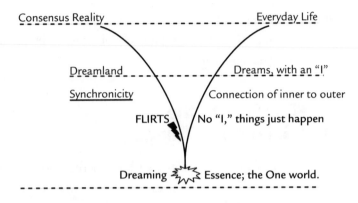

Figure 27. Flirts in the spectrum of awareness.

in which an inner event and an outer event have the same signifi-cance.[20] Jung wondered if synchronicities happen all the time. Today we can say yes, apparently synchronicities occur continuously—but because the premonitions and flirts that precede events are usually marginalized, we do not notice synchronicity. Yet the closer you are to the Dreaming, the more you experience synchronicity happening all the time.

The reason that synchronicities happen all the time is that the closer you are to the Dreaming—that is, the more you are a fast cat with flirts—the more you can consciously experience the intercon-

---

[20] Jung's original work on synchronicity was written with the support of Wolfgang Pauli, and completed in the 1950s just before Pauli's death. See Jung's "Synchronicity, An Acausal Connecting Principle" in his *Collected Works*, vol. 8. Since then, research on synchronicity is occurring at the Von Franz Institute in Zurich. *Synchronicity,* an excellent work by the Colgate University physicist Victor Mansfield, updates Jung's and Pauli's work. An excellent paper on synchronicity from a process-oriented perspective has been written by Robbie Miller (Process Work Center of Portland, 1998). Also see my *Quantum Mind*, chapter 27, for a discussion of synchronicity in connection to the principles of relativity.

nectedness between events. When you are aware of flirts or are close to the viewpoint of the Dreaming, you sense that *the energetic quality of the flirt's essence* is nonlocal and everywhere at a given moment. This may give you the experience of interconnectedness and synchronicity.

Meaning is based on the viewpoint of the little you. When your attention is focused upon consensus reality, inner and outer events arise and seem separate. When synchronicities appear, it is as if a mystery were poking its head up into the domain of "reality." In a way, synchronicity is the Dreaming's way of reminding your everyday attention that there is a mystery, a Dreaming, to this everyday world.

The point is, not only are those coinciding inner and outer events that reach your everyday awareness synchronicities, but so is *everything you notice,* since the Dreaming-like flirts apparently precede everyday observations. Since you mostly marginalize flirts, it looks as if synchronicity is an amazing and unusual experience and that dreams are foreign and unrelated to everyday life. Then, Dreaming seems to happen only at night.

When I was working as a Jungian training analyst in Zurich, I was fascinated by synchronicity and studied it in depth. No one could understand why it happened so sporadically. Now I know it doesn't. It's happening all the time.

Chang Tsu said the same thing this way: "When the body sleeps, the soul is unfolded into one. When the body wakes, the openings begin to function and many many things come out of you. But they're all one."

Things to Remember

1. Flash-flirts are evanescent observations that happen without an I, close to the Dreaming.

2. Become a lucid fast cat and catch flash-flirts. Get to their sentient essence, the Dreaming, and from there you will understand your dreams.

9

Dreamwork, Prayer, and Nonlocality

In this chapter, I return to the nature of the fast cat and the mouse to show how the mouse (that is, the content of flash-flirts) is an answer to your unformulated prayers. Knowing this will extend what you already know about dreamwork and deepen a new kind of practice given at the end of the chapter.

The Nature of the Big You

From the viewpoint of the Big You, the intelligence behind dreams, an intelligence Einstein might have called the "Mind of God," your everyday identity, complete with its critics and the rest of the figures in your dreams, is a momentary expression of the Dreaming.

The Big You rarely appears in the form of a particular figure. Its presence is more like sugar in tea—you can't see the sugar directly;

you only become aware of it in the overall taste. You can feel the Big You within observation, everything that catches your attention; the Big You is a basic, overall tendency toward completeness and democracy. It is in everything you do and dream, even though you may not see It personified as a figure.

Like the quantum world that has a nonlocal quality to it, your Big You is not entirely separate from my Big You. Connecting to your deepest feelings, your Dreaming, connects you to others. The Big You is the invisible background to community.

If love means openness to whatever is happening, then the Big You is unconditional love. It seems to me that the Big You loves "this" and It also loves "that," and It even loves the conflict between the two. The little me is very different. I usually prefer this to that and avoid conflict if I can!

The Content of Flash-Flirts

Flash-flirts are the earliest signs we perceive of the Dreammaker's expressions unfolding into everyday consciousness. From the viewpoint of the little you, flash-flirts are surprising and, at first, apparently meaningless events whose significance can easily be overlooked.

One of my clients, who works in a small office in the city, told me that during her coffee break one morning, she went to the refrigerator (as she usually did every morning), to get some milk for coffee for herself and her colleagues. When she opened the small refrigerator in her office, one of her office colleagues commented on the smell of cake and then, everyone present nodded and murmured their agreement on the pleasant smell of cake coming from that refrigerator. Everyone started talking about the cake without even seeing it. They assumed that this unseen cake must be for someone's birthday—but it wasn't anybody's birthday.

From the viewpoint of everyone's little you in that office, cake was a good smell—but certainly not something to focus on, not in the morning, and especially since it was no one's birthday. Furthermore, there was no actual real cake in that refrigerator! The perception of cake had been a flirt picked up by one person, who mentioned it, and then everyone joined in the perception of the flirt.

My client was very interested in psychology and very fascinated by flirts, so instead of dropping the issue, she picked it up again. She told everyone that this nonexistent cake was exactly what she had been praying for unconsciously. She wanted to sweeten the atmosphere in that office. She commented on the fact that no one had been celebrated for quite a while.

Apparently the business she worked for had been losing money and everyone was nervous and unhappy. People were afraid of losing their jobs. The chocolate cake flirt was a kind of answer to an unformulated prayer: "Dear God, please make life at work a bit sweeter!" This was a prayer that no one had consciously uttered. Yet all the people in her office were hoping for a birthday, a rebirth.

At first, my client's colleagues did not know what she was talking about when she said that the cake was an answer to a prayer. But when she proceeded to spend the coffee break praising everyone and wishing them happy birthday, everyone's mood changed for the better.

Figure 28. The flirting birthday cake.

The generalization from this story is that flirts are the answers to prayers that have not yet been formulated. They are messages, sent by Dreaming to the little you and to everything and everyone around you. In the last chapter, we saw how flash-flirts can create a direct connection into the Dreaming. Now, from the viewpoint of the little you, we will explore how *flash-flirts are answers to unformulated prayers*.

Most of us have unformulated prayers in the form of deep longings and unanswered existential questions. Such prayers are rarely consciously thought about; they are usually marginalized. Some prayers are for the well-being of others; other prayers are for our own well-being and long life and, perhaps, becoming rich, wise, and successful. Other prayers are asking nature about what She wants from us.

Let's formulate a hypothesis that can be tested later in an exercise:

The content of the flash-flirt is the answer to a prayer that you haven't prayed for consciously. The flash-flirt is a direct link with the Dreaming.

Before we test this, let's think about some of the many different ways in which flirts manifest in our attention.

Kinds of Flirts

Flirts are signals that occur so quickly, you tend to ignore them, or mistake their content. Flirts are close to Dreaming, and you need to be a fast cat to catch them. I will list some of them below, and afterward, show how to work with them.

Visual flirts. Some flirts occur in the form of very rapid visual fantasies such as imaginations about people you know. They also can appear in the form of visual sensations such as the sudden brightening or dimming of your vision, as if the light were growing brighter or dimmer. The experience of seeing variations in brightness may be related to vascular spasms of the vessels carrying blood in the brain. Sometimes these spasms can indicate preclot conditions, but they can also be simple, momentary spasms or premigraine headaches. Notice these flirts, hold on to their sensations, and don't just drop them.

Smell. Remember the cake. Flirts appear in the smells that flicker by your nose. I remember once when my practice smelled like a hospital ward. I don't like that smell much, but remembered it and shared the idea of a hospital with my next client. She did not think my office smelled like a hospital, but did tell me she was wondering whether she should go to the hospital to have a cancer removed. She hoped (prayed?) that I would know what to do. Thinking of the flirt, I was able to tell her to go to the hospital. The point is, note flickering smells, hold on to their sensations, and don't just drop them.

Proprioceptive flirts. Sudden body sensations of being hot, cold, comfortable, or tense are proprioceptive flirts. Sometimes they appear as the transient sense of pressure, energy, or lack of energy that quickly passes. I once encouraged someone to notice that he was always taking a deep breath. He told me he did that because of a fleeting sensation of being under pressure—and the breath relieved that sensation. When he focused on the pressure, he realized it was a pressure from within himself, wanting to burst out to be free. He told me that freedom was his greatest wish. The point is, please notice proprioceptive flirts, hold on to body sensations, and don't just drop them.

Movement flirts. The flickering sense of a tremor, twitch, or shaking is a movement flirt. Sudden sense of dizziness or faintness is a flirt. A sense of stiffness that comes and goes is an extremely interesting sensation to work with, especially when it is a flickering experience. Sudden near slips and accidents are also flickering experiences. Notice these rapid flirts, hold on to their sensations, and don't just drop them.

Relationship flirts. Sudden thoughts about people, or finding yourself in the midst of a fantasy about someone—but the fantasy is so quick and so absurd that you forget it—is a kind of flirt. When you're in close relationship with somebody, pay attention to the forbidden thoughts that come in the form of impressions about his or her appearance, or voice. Even your perception of the person's age can flirt with you; he or she can look suddenly younger or older. Perhaps something about the other person seems new or unusual; perhaps you see auras around him. Notice these flirts, hold on to their sensations, and don't just drop them.

Sound. What kinds of sounds flicker and fade away? Notice how your own voice sounds to you; notice how the voices of others sound to you. Voice tones and inner dreaming may be connected. For example, a low-sounding voice may signal a depression. A moment of misspeaking that is quickly forgotten again is a flirt. Some people walk around with music in their heads all the time. Do you? The point is: Notice these flirts, hold on to their sensations, and don't just drop them.

The Prayer-Flirt-Dreamwork Exercise

In the following exercise, I want to test the hypothesis that flirts are answers to unformulated prayers and also help to explain dreams. Part A of the following exercise explores the significance of flirts. In part B, we will integrate flirts with dreamwork.

A. Flirts and Prayer

1. The first part of this exercise is simply to relax. Close your eyes, notice the rhythm of your breathing. Wait until you are ready, and then slowly open your eyes and gaze around the area or room you are in.

Notice what catches your eye—an image, shape, object, or a person—or as an alternative, what sensation catches your body sense, movement sense, relationship fantasy sense, or sense of smell. Let your unconscious mind determine what to focus on. Catch and hold one thing in your mind's eye, for example, an object near you in your room—say, a round vase. Again, if you catch many things, ask the Dreammaker what to focus on, let your unconscious mind tell you what is most important. Describe the flirt that caught your attention. (For example, if a vase caught your attention, describe it here.)

Now unfold that flirt. Hold it in your mind, look at it, feel it; if you can, perhaps even smell it. Could it, or does it, make a sound? Does it have some very subtle movement associated with it? What movements, if any, might it make, or what movement does it invoke in you? (For example, perhaps the vase gives you the sense of roundness and balance and you feel an urge to begin to sit like a Buddha, with a big round belly, in a lotus position.) Describe the process of unfolding your flirt.

2. To get to the essence of that flirt, sense the energy and movement it evokes in you. Experience the presence of that object or figure that caught your attention, now try to be it, and move or sit the way it does. Continue to be and move in the way it does. It might help you to move just a bit less, to get to the essence of that figure, the essence of the flirt. Finally, don't move at all, but simply feel "its" energy. Give yourself a moment to do this. Feel and sense this essence, this Dreaming. Let it "speak" to you, perhaps as a picture, as a sentence, or sound.

Ask this Dreaming if It has a message for you. What is this message for you in this experience? Don't work hard at this, let it be easy. Just let a message come to mind; don't try to *think* what it might be. Remember that message. (For example, the vase's message might be something like, "Be round. Detach from the viewpoint of the little you.") Make a note about your message.

3. If you believe in a God or Goddess, or a Great Spirit—call it whatever you want—experiment with praying to this deity. If you do not hold such a belief, pretend that you do. Take time with this. What would you pray for today? Feel into your heart and actually talk to the Great Spirit and pray for something. Are you worried about health, money, relationships, your role in life, your education, and your path in life? Whatever comes to mind first, make up a simple prayer and write it down. (For example, you might write something like "Dear god, please tell me how to relate to Sam, a friend of mine.")

4. Now recall the message you received from the flirt. If you cannot directly notice the connection between your message and your prayer, consider the possibility that the message from the Dreaming concerned the deeper nature of your prayer; that the Dreaming was dealing with the basic issue behind your prayers.

   After pondering your prayers and the message from the Dreaming, finally ask yourself, in what manner does the message from your flirt answer your prayers? Make a note about that now.

The Dreaming is trying to speak to you all day long. The things that catch your attention are the answers to prayers you haven't quite formulated. People always ask where is the Great Spirit, where is God, why doesn't She show Herself more to me? Consider the possibility that She does manifest Herself to you; however, the answers are so quick, you may not spot them. That's why you have to become a fast cat!

Remember the message you just experienced in unfolding your flirt because it will be part of the next step in dreamwork. You will be able to integrate storytelling with the message of the flirt you just received.

B. Dreamwork Tale and Flirt

Recall a recent short dream or the fragment of any dream that now comes to mind.

Notice the dream figures and the relationships between them.

Is the Big You present as a figure or a dream landscape? If so, what does It look like?

1. Gather associations to the figures and landscapes in your dream. For the remainder of the exercise, the word "figure" is used to refer to any aspect of the dream—be it a person, object, creature, landscape—that catches your attention. I symbolize these *figures* with the little round faces.

   Choose one or two figures and notice your associations.

Personal association to , that is figure 1.

Personal association to , that is figure 2.

Pop-up association to , figure 1.

Pop-up association to , figure 2.

Collective information about , figure 1.

Collective information about , figure 2.

Gather information about everyday life. Ask about the role played by the little you in life. Make a note of that now.

Ask about problems and issues concerning work, age,

identity, economics, health, gender, race, religion, sexual orientation, and so forth.

Age
Gender
Race
Identity
Health
Sexual orientation
Relationships
Work
Finances
Does the dreamer have a connection to something meaningful in life?

2. Notice Big You information. What moods or feelings have been present during recent days that have been too common, comfortable, or uncomfortable to focus on?
Comfortable moods
Uncomfortable moods

Remember the energy and the message from the flirt you experienced in part A of this exercise.

3. Co-create a fabulous, dreamlike story. If you are working alone, you can co-create in the sense of recognizing and exploring how the spontaneous nature of Dreaming can weave stories, together with your assistance of your conscious mind. In what happens next, you will be invited to feel, and experience an altered state of consciousness by sensing the time and space of the Dreaming behind your flirt and its message. Then you will be encouraged to weave together your everyday problems and your associations to your dream figures. If you are working with someone else, encourage him or her to do the same, that is, to co-create with you.

To begin with, recall and feel once again the world of that flirt you noticed in part A. Now try to use the energy of its world, its mood or atmosphere to weave a story involving the everyday problems of the dreamer. For example:

> *Once upon a time, in another region of the world, some years back, there was a person who was working on a problem about . . . That person would always get tied up with certain problems such as . . . What a time she or he had trying to solve them. Her age, which was . . . and her role in life, which was . . . did not really help her with this problem. What she needed was not immediately apparent.*

Now continue to feel and speak in the tone and rhythm of the Dreaming behind the flirt. Weave in the dream figures. For example:

> *At the same time in her area were the following objects and landscape (choose some from the dream). . . . In her area there lived the following dream figures. . . . She had the following associations to them. . . . These figures had the same problems as she did, or else were free of these problems.*

Add the message from the flirt into the story.

> *At a given point in this tale, a prayer emerged. Our heroine fell on her knees and begged the Great Spirit for a favor. Please, God, help me with . . . She was patient and waited several hours until darkness occurred. Then, suddenly, she heard an uncanny sound, and an answer, a voice, which said [include here the message from the flirt]. It was as if the earth or sky spoke, and when It said . . . The person who had just prayed was amazed and shocked at first. She could not see how that message would help her. It seemed right but not directly related to her problems. And*

> *then the voice spoke again and explained Itself. This time, she got
> it . . . she knew the Great Spirit wanted her to . . .*

If the dreamer got the point, that is the end of the story. If she
did not, try embellishing the message of the Dreaming by letting
yourself dream on. Continue telling that story until the dreamer
and heroine in the story are both content.

4. Retell the story, stressing the marginalized flirts, the dream figures, and the everyday problems. Emphasize the amazing way in
   which the prayers were answered, and what that meant for the
   various figures in the story. Ponder the story that just created
   itself; listen to the Dreaming oracle.

   You may want to ask why the heroine needed to have prayers
   answered in the first place. Was she inadvertently marginalizing
   the Dreaming, making it impossible for It to speak or be heard?
   As far as I know, when you are deeply aware of, and responsive
   to, the Dreaming, prayers—the need for answers to problems—
   do not arise within you because most problems are caused by
   marginalization of the Dreaming.

Nature is amazing. She has arranged existence in such a way that
when you have lost contact with the Dreaming, It can be found right
in front of you, so to speak. Then, when you are not connected to
the Dreaming, every sudden perception, every flirt is the potential
answer to a prayer.

Music and Dance from the 1920s

For example, a movement flirt—a slight tremor—was always dis-
tracting one of my first clients, an older woman with whom I worked
years ago. To make the story short, she had been worried about having

enough energy to finish the things she wanted to do in life. Her prayer was, "Please God, give me the energy to finish up my project." Then she noticed the slight tremor in her hand. I still remember her beginning to move with that flirt. She noticed that her hand was trying to dance to a tune from the 1920s. What a happy tune she sang!

The message from this flirt was "Enjoy the rhythm of life." Apparently she had been pushing herself to do her project, and marginalized the rhythm and happy dance of life. Before even co-creating a story with me, she understood the meaning of a dream she had had the night before. In her dream, a woman had fallen to the ground. "I am pushing too hard," she said.

In any case, in the mood of that rhythm and dance, she happily made up a story of a woman who was always pushing herself, and had fallen to the ground out of exhaustion. In her story, the Great Spirit spoke from the ground to her saying, "Hey, friend, have a good time. There is plenty of dance energy to swing through any project." At that point in the story she got up and danced. At the time of this dreamwork she was eighty-nine. She lived another ten years, and during that time wrote and published her first book.

Why Do We Marginalize the Dreaming?

A question that used to bother me is, why does the Dreaming create a little you, the person who needs to pray because she or he has fallen out of contact with the inner oracle? If you were the Dreaming, why would You create something that forgets You, that is so different from, or even antagonistic to You?

My answer to this question today is that the Dreaming is very wise. Perhaps It creates consensus reality and the limited and often insensitive nature of folks like you and me who marginalize the Dreaming in order to experience Itself by contrast. To see Itself, the Dreaming needs a contrasting background.

Perhaps that is why It arises from the depths, and simultaneously marginalizes awareness of Its own arising by creating individuals like you and me who move in fixed, established ways that dismiss, overlook, or ignore the ongoing, ever-changing nature of the Dreaming process. Dreaming becomes apparent only when juxtaposed with Its opposite—the more or less fixed background of everyday life.

The consensus reality part of you and me resists Dreaming. We often feel that Its creativity is too subtle, outrageous, intrusive, and unfair, too irrational, and much too unresponsive to our sense of identity as ordinary human beings.

At the same time, there is another part of us that longs for the Dreaming to win the battle between stasis and change—between the static, fixed background of everyday life and the eternally fluid, ongoing process that is the life source. What we perceive to be an outrageous dichotomy between the nonlocal Dreaming essence and the marginalizing, localized, body-oriented, everyday little you and little me is perhaps not a dichotomy after all. From the Dreaming perspective, this apparent dichotomy is simply two different manifestations of the same picture, the same story, the same essence appearing in a fabulous story called "Your Life."

 Things to Remember

1. Flirts and dreams are the answer to prayers that have not been formulated or even thought.

2. The little you and the Big You belong to each other—and together, the combination creates an outrageous story.

4

EVERYDAY LIFE AS A DREAM

Interpreting Dreams of Nondreamers

10

Secret Dreaming for Nondreamers

Dreamwork is an artistic act that cannot be pinned down with a fixed methodology. The exercises in this book are simply suggestions. They are meant to train your awareness, not to be used as rules. The methods that arise in working with yourself or others depend entirely on the moment, and on your nature and theirs. Once you learn some basic tools, your own Dreaming will take over, and dreamwork will become an art.

Being able to focus on the present moment gives you the ability to work not only with people who have dreams, but also with folks who do not believe that they dream. Before exploring how to work with nondreamers, I want to review the material covered thus far; then we will explore the interconnections among dreams, Dreaming, and what Jung called the "archetypes."

Brief Review

The problem with working on dreams by yourself is that dreamwork requires relativity; we are often too close to ourselves and our dreams to see the larger picture. The solution that I have presented in this book is to gain distance from our ordinary minds by accessing Dreaming, the central (or at least one of the central) altered states of consciousness. Through the sense of Dreaming, we know where our dreams come from and are less surprised and overwhelmed by them.

In part 1, we explored gaining access to the Dreaming by quieting the everyday mind through breathing meditations and then noticing how images and events arise, first in the Dreaming flow; then via shapes, figures, and landscapes in Dreamland; and then through myriad experiences of everyday reality. Focusing on the rhythm of your breathing, counting each exhalation up to ten, and then noticing the sentient experience that arises give you an empirical experience of how dreams arise spontaneously.

We differentiated the psychological interpretation of dreams, which deals with parts and their relationship to the little you, from the spiritual interpretation that involves awareness of being a host or even apprentice to the Dreammaker.

In part 2, we explored the spontaneous nature of symbols and identified the types of associations we make in response to these symbols: personal, relational, pop-up, and collective associations. We explored going into an altered state directed by the time and space of the dreamer's present moods, and we discussed how to access the dreamer's ally and its wisdom.

In part 3, we focused on becoming a "fast cat" to catch that divine mouse, that is, a flirt. Now, in part 4, we will explore how everyday life is itself a dream.

What Are Archetypes?

When I first began to study psychology in the mid-1960s, I had just completed my studies in applied physics and could not quite understand why you needed to study archetypes, myths, and fairy tales to understand dreams. People themselves create myths and tales. Nevertheless, I realized at that time, and still feel today, that archetypes, myths, and fairy tales are fabulous things to study.

Each culture co-creates its myths—stories coming from its Dreaming. Myths are examples not only of two people working on a dream, but of the co-creative process of thousands and even millions of beings. However, a problem with collective myths and fairy tales is that they contain many examples of marginalizations and edges.

Some kinds of individuals and dreamlike figures are allowed, others are repressed. The pictures of the dreamworld we find in dreams and myths contain mysteries, facts, and also prejudices. Myths and tales do hint at the Dreaming, and also at marginalizations that give rise to such cultural problems as racism, sexism, and homophobia.

Jung felt there were archetypes that created thematic patterns or blueprints that cultures used in their stories. The details of the stories vary from culture to culture, but the underlying structures of the stories are remarkably similar. According to Jung, "Archetypes intervene in the shaping of conscious contents by regulating, modifying and motivating them."[21] Dreams are structured by mythological motifs that describe "in the best possible way the dimly discerned nature of the spirit . . . and point beyond to a meaning that is darkly divined yet still beyond our grasp."[22]

---

[21]See Jung's *The Collected Works,* vol. 8, paragraph 404.
[22]See Jung's *The Collected Works,* vol. 8, paragraph 644.

Jung's concept of the archetypes is analogous to how I think of quantum physics and elementary particles.[23] In quantum physics, things are neither waves nor particles, although our consensus reality ideas make us think of them in these terms. Elementary "particles" behave like nothing else you have ever experienced in everyday life. They are not really particles, this quantum stuff. The term "particle" is a learned, consensual term referring to something localized at a given point in space and time. The idea of an elementary particle merely points to the quantum world, which is essentially nonlocal and nontemporal, and whose appearance in everyday reality depends in great part on how we look at it.

The Dreaming is similar. When you are close to the Dreaming, the locality of where you experience yourself to be is no longer certain in terms of space or time. Furthermore, what you notice in this world, as it arises into Dreamland and everyday reality, greatly depends on how open you are to the arising experiences and to your personal "dictionary" of descriptions. Therefore, it makes sense that the archetypal images found in Dreamland, such as the King and the Queen, and so on, have nonlocal and universal qualities.

Jung saw the archetypes as the primordial patterns behind images, universal models found in everyone and expressed everywhere in mythology, literature, and the arts. Archetypes pattern our commonly shared experiences such as confronting death, falling in love, becoming whole, and the like. Jung found symbols of these events, such as the grim reaper, Eros, and wisdom figures, in religions, myths, fantasies, and fairy tales.

We need to ask ourselves again and again about the nature of dream images, archetypes, Dreaming, and "the unconscious," not

---

[23]This analogy and discussion of archetypes and particles was inspired by private correspondence with the Canadian physicist, Professor Charles Card.

necessarily to answer our questions definitively, but rather to remind ourselves that our approach to dreams depends entirely on what we think they are. For example, if you think of the unconscious as manifesting itself mainly in the form of nighttime dreams, you tend to get bored with someone who does not dream. I know from supervising dreamworkers who focus mainly on dreams that they often get bored and feel something is not quite right with people who do not dream much.

From the viewpoint of Dreaming, archetypes don't exist; they are merely the momentary patterns of energies, names that people use to formulate the tendencies of Dreaming. These tendencies are nonlocal and nontemporal; they happen everywhere, and constantly, not only at night. To understand archetypal patterns better, perhaps it is helpful to remember sand patterns made on the beach as water from a lake or sea washes ashore. Archetypes are like sand formations on the beach near the ocean. As the water flows in, the sand takes on particular forms. However, in time, the whole beach is changed by the nature of the ebbing and flowing water. *Seen over time, archetypes are* not static forms but *shifting tendencies* resulting from the interaction between water and land.

If your viewpoint is that of a moment on the beach, then for brief periods forms and archetypes exist. You name those patterns in the terms of your personal understanding and experiences.[24] However, if your viewpoint moves with the water, forms are constantly changing and nothing is true for more than an instant. From the viewpoint of Dreaming, the ever-changing patterns attributable to the interaction between Dreaming and everyday life are awesome: the perpetually changing awesomeness is the point.

---

[24]Thanks to Richard Leviton for pointing out that Westerners, Hindus, Chinese, and others have different expressions for star constellations. For example, Hindus see an antelope whereas Westerners see Orion.

The moral of the story is that there are various ways of seeing dreams. If you are fascinated by the images, you see archetypes, and the Dreaming becomes an enigmatic message from the "unconscious." Then, if a person reports no images from the night, you assume there was no dream. If you experience the altered states of consciousness connected to the Dreaming, however, images become less significant than the *sense of eternal change and the energy of impermanence.*

From the viewpoint of Dreaming, even when nothing appears in Dreamland, even when you cannot remember a dream at night, the Dreaming is still there, showing itself in the here and now—in the energy behind the feelings, fantasies, body problems, smells, and tastes that make up everyday life. Just as time goes on, Dreaming happens all the time and is everywhere, always.

What Is Right about Not Dreaming at Night?

Before concentrating on the skills needed to notice the Dreaming in everyday life, let me briefly share with you some of the possible reasons I have heard from people for not remembering dreams.

• Not Interested: Some people say they are not interested in dreams, so why remember them?

• Too Vague: Some people say their dreams are too cloudy, too vague.

• Medications: Some medications obscure dreams.

• Fear: Some people have told me, "I'm afraid of my dreams—they're going to show how bad I am or they're going to scare me. I hate my nightmares." These dreamers feel that not dreaming is a way of fighting a negative or even frightening inner critic. (Such dreamers remind me to use a more spiritual approach to dreaming that does not criticize the dreamer or prescribe methods intended to help them "grow.")

• Can't Remember: Some say they can't remember anything. Memory is a fascinating and complex topic. Many people are nervous about the loss of their memory. (Sometimes the fear of this loss is very unconscious, and people smoke instead, to stimulate their memory—but using nicotine is not the best method of awakening memory.) I try to understand the significance of memory loss. It often seems that when the Big You is not interested in something, your memory begins to give you trouble.

Learning about Dreaming from People in Extreme States

I have learned a lot about Dreaming from people who are in extreme states of consciousness, more commonly called "chronic psychotic states." When I began to work with my first clients in Zurich in the late 1960s, interest in and the use of medication were not as prevalent as they are today. This lack of medication gave me the chance to work with a number of people in extreme states of consciousness. In those states, people merge reality and Dreaming and show how to dream without inhibiting it.

I have learned a lot from observing, exploring, and joining in their experiences, and realize how helpful the essence of an extreme state can be for someone in an ordinary state of consciousness. In fact, if I feel blocked from my Dreaming, I sometimes ask myself, what I would experience now if I allowed myself to be psychotic? What extreme state would I go into?

Extreme States and Dreamwork

If you feel safe enough with your own tendencies toward extreme behavior, get to know it better by trying the following exercise:

1. Take a moment and ask yourself right now: If you were able to go into an extreme state of consciousness—if you were to "go crazy"—what state would you enter into? Imagine that state now.

2. What do you see and feel yourself doing? Give yourself some time, and allow yourself to experience it.

3. Do you notice how the experience of this state brings some sort of relief to your conscious mind? It often seems as if such states have been struggling to reach your everyday awareness.

4. Explore that "psychotic" state and imagine what you would do in that state.

When your experience of that state has unfolded itself in your imagination, recall a recent dream, and try to understand that dream from the perspective of this altered state of consciousness induced by working with your extreme state.

Extreme states are very close to Dreaming and may help you understand yourself better. I recall a very creative but troubled client from Switzerland who said that she "never" dreamed. However, she came to me because her doctor said that she was chronically hallucinating; nevertheless, she was more or less able to get along in the day, and often spent her time wandering through the streets of Zurich in a very altered state of consciousness. She kept telling everyone around her that the police department had arrested four Swiss on the Niederdorfstrasse in downtown Zurich. (That is the old town of Zurich, filled with lots of nightlife—theater, bars, etc.)

One day during an office visit, she was in a very excited mood, speaking to me continuously without hesitating, telling me that the "cops are arresting drunks here on the Niederdorfstrasse. In fact, the birds are flying over the church steeple and squawking, squawk, squawk, and squawk. Do you [Arny] not see them? The birds squawk all day and all night long, after the drunks are arrested in the bar."

She was mixing Dreaming and reality. My office was not on the Niederdorfstrasse; there were no real cops, no real drunks, and no birds in my office. Yet in Dreamland she was right there with the cops, drunks, and birds.

To work with such a creative person, I tried to be at least as creative as she was. My client said, "Ah, oh, the police are awful, I see them arresting four people on the Niederdorfstrasse in Zurich. Birds are flying over the church and they squawk, squawk. The cops are arresting drunks on the Niederdorfstrasse. The cops come and those birds go squawk, squawk."

I joined in saying that "the birds went *squawk* because they are above and beyond the cops and the drunks. The birds are squawking! The birds can see it all, they have the overview. Can you hear the birds talking to the police? I hear them."

My client replied to me, "They go squawk." Laughing loudly she said, "Yes! They are above it all."

I felt encouraged and went further with the story, intermingling my own guesses at the significance of her tale. "The birds squawk and are telling the cops to lay off. Listen here, cops, we feel that it is okay to be an ecstatic, a nut, and a drunk!" To keep things in balance, I spoke for the cops as well. "But the cops yelled out, 'No, you have to go to work, you can't be a crazy nut all the time!'" Getting excited about this Dreaming—which was now mine as well—I plunged forward, saying, "The drunks screamed back at the cops, 'Let us be crazy, we *are* nuts!'"

At this point my client shocked me by sharply intervening in the midst of this fantasy conflict. Speaking up, taking the side of the police, she scolded me, "Stop those drunks! The cops are right! If the drunks are not careful, they will have to go to the mental hospital." At this point the dreamer became the police and told me, "You are drunk and should 'sober up.'" In reality, this sobered up both of us, and my client felt better.

For the moment, I was more grounded, and she too became more grounded in everyday reality. Perhaps my client's problem was that the world around her was too sober. When I took up the role of the ecstatic drunk, she could be the cop and come back to "normal."[25]

This dreamer was a highly intelligent person. I assumed that her extreme state was just another form of Dreaming. The Big You in her knew exactly what It was doing. There is no pathology from the viewpoint of the Dreammaker. It was trying to unfold Itself in terms of the agony of marginalizing altered states of consciousness.

To make the story brief, within a year she learned to live that ecstatic state in reality. I joined her in her creativity, in Dreaming, and wove the birds together with the cops and the drunks. She never told me a dream because, for her, everyday reality was full of dreams.

---

[25]I speak at greater length in *City Shadows: Psychological Interventions in Psychiatry,* about how to intervene in creative ways without medication. Such intervention requires experience with the Dreaming and with people in all sorts of states of consciousness.

If you want to work with someone who says they don't dream, a useful intervention—if they are not afraid of extreme states—is to ask them to experience being "crazy" for a short period of time, to get to the Dreamland in everyday reality.

Dreamdoors

Dreaming does not happen only in extreme states, but also can be seen to enter everyday life in ordinary states of consciousness through events I call "dreamdoors." All the things people say and do during the day that catch our attention are dreamlike. If people dream, you will find these things in nighttime dreams.

Therefore, I call those events (like the cops, the drunks, and the birds) that catch and hold our attention "dreamdoors." A dreamdoor is a potential opening to another world, another realm. It is a door, an opening, an invitation that can be taken, or not.

Figure 29. An open dreamdoor (for a Western person).

If you open and go through a dreamdoor, you get a new view of a reality. If you go through that door, your space and time change.

For example, the use of the future or past tense in a sentence is a door through which dreams may enter. Make a note when dreamers speak about events as if they were not present in the here and now but occurring in the past or in the future or in another place. Dreamland appears in narratives in terms of past, future, or not here, not-me.

One of my clients once insisted that he had not remembered his dreams for a long time. So I asked him what he did yesterday, thinking perhaps his use of the past tense would be a dreamdoor into his Dreaming process. He told me that "yesterday was Sunday and our whole family went on an outing, but I wanted to stay home. I felt lazy, like nothing mattered. I had nothing to do and felt more relaxed than normal. I just loved hanging around at home."

I thought he was Dreaming about "hanging around" and doing nothing and suggested that he go through the dreamdoor of "feeling relaxed yesterday" by exploring that feeling now, today, in the moment. He gladly did that, and for at least five minutes looked like he had sunk into a meditation. Suddenly he opened his eyes and said, "Wow, I just remembered a dream I had last night of going underwater." His experience of Dreaming brought back the nighttime dream and the interpretation. He was a host to the experience of deep meditation. The psychological interpretation was that he needed to have more relaxation and inwardness in everyday life.

Secret Dreamwork

If you listen closely to yourself and others as they tell you about what they are thinking, you can do a sort of "secret dreamwork." Secret dreamwork focuses on everyday life as a dream, without the dreamer being lucid that she is dreaming and working on her dream.

In the preceding case, the secret dreamwork was noticing the dreamdoor, the use of the past tense in connection with "relaxation," or "hanging around," and going through that door to interpret a dream that had not yet been reported or remembered.

Secret dreamwork consists in listening closely for events happening in:

• The past
• The future
• Not-here places
• Not-me people, objects, or situations

To train yourself in using this method, I suggest that you try the following exercise:

1. Ask yourself or another dreamer to tell you stories about yesterday and about things that happened then. These stories will be full of figures from everyday life—friends, enemies, allies, attackers, and perhaps even altered states of consciousness.

   If you develop the right listening skills, the dreamer will feel free to tell you more about the events from yesterday and even explore them with you. This is secret dreamwork in the sense that the dreamer may not yet be aware that she or he is speaking about dreams. You must maintain your awareness in this exercise and not get hypnotized by thinking that yesterday is only yesterday and not Dreaming. At first, it helps to listen to the stories of the dreamer and write them down in order to dream on.

   While the person is telling a given story, you can sense the power of Dreaming in the feeling or atmosphere used in telling the story.

2. When the dreamer is truly involved in telling the story, it is a living presence for her or him, a Dreaming. Feel into that Dreaming and use that energy to dream on!

   For example, one dreamer told me about having gone to a doctor's appointment yesterday, so I joined her in that story. I asked her, "What happened then? What did the doctor do? Oh, the doctor tested you for allergies? Fascinating. Did you say you were not sure about taking that medication for your allergies? Why are you not taking that medication?" At this point the dreamer said that she felt she needed something special, something more than medicine for allergies, something deeper, because her "allergies felt so weird" to her.

   Later she read me a dream from her dream book. "I dreamed I was getting special medication for something from someone called a tree doctor."

I don't want to go further with that particular dreamwork here. I just want to indicate how the use of the past tense can be a dreamdoor. In this case, yesterday's visit to the doctor was a dreamdoor that I went through to do secret dreamwork by empathetically joining the dreamer in her story.

While doing secret dreamwork, remember other things you have learned as well. Watch the dreamer closely. Do flirts distract her or him? If there are flirts that pop up while you are doing this work, all the better. Bring them in as well.

In doing secret dreamwork, you should try to enter a slightly altered state of consciousness together with the dreamer. You need a gossiplike style, which is experimental, free, and compassionate. You can tell the dreamer that you are doing secret dreamwork, or you can simply begin to join in by embellishing her or his tale. Try to get information about the figures and stories the dreamer tells you, and then you can begin weaving a tale based on yesterday's experiences.

Gathering information about dreamdoors is more like gossip than like gathering associations from someone reporting a nighttime dream. You can even add elements that were not part of the dreamer's story, such as wise, helpful allies. Perhaps the hints given in the following exercise will be helpful.

Secret Dreaming Exercise

1. Talk about yesterday, and listen for the tone of the story. Notice what excites the dreamer—the terror, boredom, excitement, passion, fatigue, or depression with which the dreamer speaks. That is part of the Dreaming. Emotional moments are dreamdoors: Go through them!

2. Notice with whom the person identifies; for example, the first client I mentioned above was identified with the drunks. Or notice the figures with whom the dreamer sides.

3. Listen for figures the dreamer likes least. In the case of that client, the cops were least liked in the beginning.

4. If a wise figure or state of mind was present, use that as an ally in the eventual story you create together. If you can't find such a figure and would like one to be present, ask the dreamer to add a helpful animal into the story. This is especially useful in working with kids, but it is good for everyone.

5. Relax, be creative, and let the different elements of the dreamer's story come to life as they weave themselves together. Tell stories. Get the other to co-create with you.

Here are some "stories of yesterday" told by people in one of my classes. These stories are very brief and are only meant to give you a hint about getting started in storytelling with dream-doors.

Ellen: Yesterday I spent three hours in the editing room and I couldn't achieve what I needed to achieve. That's . . . depressing.

Arny: Oh, that is a depressing story. It is enough to make a normal person give up on life! Thank god a helpful animal suddenly appeared in that editing room at the right moment.

Ellen: A hedgehog![26]

Arny: A hedgehog, with all its spikes? In an editing room? Of course. Just think about what it did!

Ellen: Um, I was in the damn editing room, frustrated as hell. Then came the hedgehog and it shrugged off all its sharp bits. Prickles. It, threw them off. Yeah. And anyone who was around got one. Right in the ass!

Arny: Oh, and anyone who was around got one of these sharp things from the animal. In fact, a damn critic who was standing around, making all sorts of stupid comments, got one of those stingers right in his ass, and he screamed so loud he ran away and never came back.

Ellen: Right on. That critic had been telling that editor to not follow her heart but her head! End of story! I got it!

Here is another example of using dreamdoors and secret dreaming.

---

[26]The hedgehog is a relative of the mole and is covered with long, pointed spines, except on its underbelly, where it has soft fur. When threatened, hedgehogs roll into balls so their spines project in all directions.

John: I got up very early yesterday . . . and worked for a couple of hours, I had a long, hard day working. I was stuck, working on a paper on political issues.

Arny: Such a hard day must have been exhausting. Whew! It must have been almost impossible to get through that day. I would have gone to sleep

John: That's right, it *was* exhausting—but something powerful inside of me managed to get through it all. I felt stuck at my writing.

Arny: Thank god there was some helpful animal there. Something amazing, uncanny, unbelievable, almost inconceivable. Amazing!

John: There was an elephant! It was a *blue* elephant. In addition, it opened the fridge. It stuck its trunk into the fridge and sniffed. It found cheese. Boy, that was fun and it ate all that cheese.[27]

Arny: What a great smell that cheese had! Thank god that elephant was not shy about going after things that tasted good, even if they made a stink!

John: Yes. The elephant took that cheese, ate it all, and breathed into my computer, and went crazy, writing, painting, speaking the truth, which was nourishing but did not always smell good to people. The elephant was so big and so creative, it only had to breathe cheese into the computer, and the work was done. And I, the writer, felt authentic.

---

[27]Some general collective information may be helpful for some readers. Elephants are social animals and associate in small herds for protection from predators. The dominant female, or matriarch, leads each elephant family. When threatened, the members of the herd surround the calves to protect them from danger, and either the matriarch confronts the danger or the group retreats in a tight unit. I could have used the information that elephants are social animals, led by a powerful female, in my storytelling, but I did not think of it at the time of the story. Furthermore, of great importance, especially for John, would have been the information that in Hinduism, Ganesha, the great god of writing and wisdom, has an *elephant's* head!

John looked enlightened; apparently he was trying to write his paper in such a manner that everything "smelled just right."

The point is that secret dreaming can proceed by opening up the dreamdoor called "yesterday" and joining the dreamer in a story that is as real as any experience in Dreamland. Go through that dreamdoor and begin the process of weaving, connecting moods and associations, gossip and allies. Remember, we all talk about yesterday, so listen closely. The story of yesterday explains the Dreaming happening today.

Things to Remember

1. Everyone dreams, even when they don't remember dreams.

2. Listen for dreamdoors, such as references to past and future situations.

3. Be a little "crazy"; do secret dreaming by joining the "not-here," "not-now" stories. Add helpful spirits and animals.

4. See how the story of yesterday is the Dreaming of today.

11

Reality As Dream-Music

In chapter 10, I called all the things people say and do during the day that can be found in nighttime dreams "dreamdoors." Remember that a dreamdoor is a potential opening to another world, another realm. It is an invitation that can be taken or not. Dreamdoors give you a view of a separate reality. If you go through that door, your space and time change and you can do what I called "secret dreaming."

I showed how the past, future, and not-here references are dreamdoors that open to Dreamland and Dreaming. I want to discuss a whole array of such doors in this chapter, and then create an experiment using awareness of music that transforms everyday reality and Dreamland into one another.

Complexes Are Dreamdoors

Freud and Jung found dreamdoors in what they called "complexes." For example, Jung spoke in terms of a "negative mother complex" or "negative father complex." Not being cared for by your mother or father can be so traumatic that a mother or father "complex" results; then everything associated with mothering—for example, eating, caring for and liking yourself—becomes a complicated, emotional issue. When you are "in a complex," for example, in a self-deprecating mood during the day, you are likely to see this mood symbolized in your dreams at night in terms of unkind parental figures. Jung said that "complexes architect" dreams.

Any "affect" or strong, lasting emotional reaction to something during the day—something that sucks you in and from which you cannot get away—can appear in your dreams at night. There you see your father or mother, for example, or other objects and people associated directly or indirectly with the parents—filling your dreams.

Some dreamdoors, like complexes, suck you through the door and get you into states and moods you wish you could get out of! The "little you" thinks that some doors should just never be opened! Please, just leave them shut!

In any case, complexes are dreamdoors. Opening them means getting into emotional issues. Secret dreaming with complexes is like surfing high waves; complexes are a difficult form of Dreaming because we easily get swamped, sucked in, and lose awareness of what's going on. That may be why Jung and Freud suggested "analyzing" complexes, to point out what was happening to you, so that you could understand what is behind those doors while essentially keeping the door more or less shut. By analyzing complexes, you could at least talk about what you saw behind that door. If you *think* about complexes, you don't necessarily have to go directly into them, not now, at least.

However, events of everyday life reactivate complexes and open up those dreamdoors whether you are ready or not. If you have had painful or traumatic experiences, at first you may need to close the doors and leave them shut. Where trauma is located, the Big You shuts the door and does not let you think about things until you are ready to protect yourself from more trauma than you can handle.

Shamans claim that you should never go through a dreamdoor (i.e., into the unknown) without an ally who can help you in the other world. You need allies in Dreaming. Carlos Castaneda's Native American Yaqui shaman Don Juan Matus taught that you must become a warrior and learn the skills of shamanic journeying into altered states and spaces before you go through dreamdoors.[28] The exercise at the end of this chapter is a training in both the analytical and the shamanic journey techniques.

Flirts and Dreamdoors

The future and past, as well as complexes, are dreamdoors. Moreover, Dreaming uses all unintentional signals, gestures, symptoms, and uncontrolled movements as dreamdoors as well. Thus you can enter and understand dreams by observing and unfolding unintentional relationship signals, inexplicable body sensations, spontaneous and unpredictable movement tendencies, as well as addictions.[29] Indeed, the point of this chapter is that Dreaming has

---

[28]I discuss Castaneda's Don Juan stories in my *Shaman's Body*.

[29]Since I explore the how Dreaming manifests itself through the dreamdoors of body symptoms, relationship gestures, and addictions in my *Dreaming While Awake*, I will confine my comments on these topics to this footnote.

We have long known that chronic symptoms relate to childhood dreams. For example, try focusing on your nonrational sense of the energy in a symptom, the energy you feel creating that symptom (and not merely on the outer description of the symptom in terms such as "pain," "stomachache," etc.). Be sure you are dealing with the energy you sense creating the symptom, and not necessarily your response to that energy. For example, a cold makes you

no special interest in dreams—they are but one of Its many manifestations!

Although there is no fast and firm border between dreamdoors and flirts, in principle they are different. Flirts are unstable, quick experiences in everyday life. You need to be a "fast cat" to catch them. In contrast to flirts, dreamdoors have more persistence in claiming your attention over time; they are firmer signals such as sentences and words that can be easily recalled.

While dreamdoors persist as messages and signals, flirts are "presignals" and are more easily overlooked. Although dreamdoors

---

tired, but the creative energy of the cold may make your nose run. If you allow that energy (such as the irritant creating the running nose) to express itself in the form of images and sounds, you discover scenes found in dreams. I called this discovery the "dreambody." For more on this topic, see my books *Dreambody* and *Working with the Dreaming Body*.

Consider the possibility that addictive tendencies, like symptoms, are also dreamdoors. A substance addiction—that is, any substance that threatens your health or relationships and which you must take more of to gain the same effect—is associated with the need for a specific change in your state of mind. If you experience that imagined, changed state of mind and go into that state of mind *without taking the substance*, stories unfold that may also be found in your dreams. Thus addictions are dreamdoors, like symptoms and special sentences, all of which manifest the Dreaming.

Unintentional relationship signals that occur while talking with another person are also reflected in dreams (see my *Dreambody in Relationships*). Notice such dreamdoors—that is, such signals—while chatting with someone, and unfold one of them by amplifying or intensifying the signal. For example, if your body is pulling back, away from someone, try to consciously pull back and let a story unfold about a person who is doing that, and chances are, you will find that story in your dreams. Relationship signals, too, are dreamdoors!

You can understand your dreams through the unintentional movements that occur during walking. Get up and try to walk. After a minute or two, notice unintentional movement tendencies and allow these tendencies to express themselves in movement. If you unfold them into a dance or movement story, you can also find how unintentional movements are also dreamdoors for the Dreaming that explains dreams.

are more readily perceived and remembered than flirts, usually we do not focus on dreamdoors since we assume they are simply part of consensus reality. We may not realize their "doorlike" quality. We only know they are doors by testing them—by exploring sentences containing the future, the past, or complexes, to see if they set you off into Dreaming. You cannot focus on flirts in this way because you can barely see them; they happen too quickly.

In learning to work with dreamdoors, you must listen carefully while people speak, and not get hypnotized into thinking that what is said is an unalterable fact. The "past" is not unalterable, in the sense that the past is an unconscious process happening in the present, a process that can be made conscious and changed.

Older people, for example, often speak about the past. If you think in terms of dreamdoors, then the past is not just a fact, but a Dreaming process happening right now, a way of entering Dreamland. I recall an older man who bothered others in his nursing home, continuously telling them about racial harassment that happened to him in the past. He upset even people who were of the same race as he. While the stories were real and important, at the same time, they were a Dreaming happening in the moment. Those racist acts were dreamdoors.

When I told him that racist remarks had been directed to me as well, he immediately joined the story and said that I should not be a coward but should fight against those acts. I asked him how to do that. He got up for the first time, and demanded new kinds of treatment in that nursing home! Until that time, I did not realize that people were treating him badly and were ignoring him because his memory was failing.

In any case, when you are awake and perceptive, dreamdoors give you the opportunity to enter into Dreaming or into secret dreaming with a dreamer who may not be aware that she is dreaming.

Dreamdoors are persistent feelings, sentences, movements, or states of mind that have three characteristics. These are:

1. Something, someone, or some object or person who catches my attention and is "not-me."
2. A time that is "not now."
3. A place or space that is "not here."

Example of Secret Dreaming

One of my therapists, Franz Riklin, knew a lot about doing secret dreaming with dreamdoors, though he never called them that. Every time I would speak about other students at the Jung Institute in Zurich during my studies there, Riklin would comment mysteriously, "Aha. That student!" I would say "Yes, of course!" Then he would inevitably say in a secretive tone, "Well, tell me about her (or him)!" It took me a long time to realize he was doing a kind of secret dreamwork with me!

Before I got to know Riklin well, I remember telling him about my best friend, Peter, a student colleague at the Institute. Here is what happened. One afternoon I came to Riklin's office to see him for therapy. I told him I had a problem. I wanted to know why I couldn't finish my studies at the Institute. Why was I procrastinating? Riklin heard me complain about my problem but promptly said, "Oh, that is a boring problem! Who wants to think about studies? Tell me something more interesting. What's happening in real life with you these days?"

I was relieved to forget those damn studies I was supposed to complete, and relaxed. We began gossiping, and I told him I loved being around my friend, another student, called Peter. I explained that Peter had the most unbelievable ability to play with ideas. He easily became bored in academic classes when teachers spoke of things that he could read in books. Peter always provoked his teachers by mumbling about their boring ideas while they were lecturing. He was more courageous than I, telling the teachers they were too lazy to develop their own theories. Peter's outspoken nature always got him into trouble.

In any case, I told Riklin that one day after class, I had lunch with Peter, and we laughed about those teachers and about everyone else. Finally, when we had finished berating everyone, we would begin to speak about very interesting subjects.

At this point in my story, Riklin asked with curiosity, "Aha! What were those really interesting topics?" I said, "Synchronicity!" Riklin jumped and said, "Aha! Fascinating! Is Peter doing a paper on that topic?" When I said, "No, that is too much work for him; he is lazy!" Riklin found the key to open my dreamdoor, the Dreaming-boring-teacher-Peter-laziness story.

Riklin pounced on the lack of creativity of the teachers, exclaiming with glee, "Aha! Peter is like those teachers who are too lazy, boring, and academic to do new and creative stuff of their own!" Then he leaned way over in his chair toward me and looked into my eyes in a very mysterious way. Out of my mouth, and against my better judgment, I heard myself clearly and slowly pronouncing, "So, I am Peter!" Riklin explained triumphantly, "Exactly!" We both laughed until tears came to my eyes.

Riklin revealed Dreaming by gossiping and then found the dreamdoors: Peter, teachers, laziness, and my own unfinished studies. He drew me into a sort of secret dreamwork that revealed both my laziness and my interest in synchronicity. That conversation with him gave me so much energy that I wrote my thesis on synchronicity and finished my studies in a few months. That's how I originally became a Jungian analyst.

The moral of my story is that dreamdoors are topics you repeat and insist upon; you think they are facts from the past or future. You do not realize they are entry points to Dreaming. Dreamdoors are tricky because they are spoken about as if they were real and not part of Dreamland. You need to remodel your hearing to catch dreamdoors. You need to listen as a dreamer listens to nighttime dreams, seeing and hearing the remarkable events trying to unfold from the Dreaming. Relate to the other person as a person with an everyday reality, and also as a dreamer in the midst of her or his apprenticeship with the Dreammaker.

A Partial List of Dreamdoors

I have already mentioned how words about yesterday that refer to the *past, the not-me, and not-here* are dreamdoors. I have indicated how *complexes* can be dreamdoors. Following are more dreamdoors:

Projections. When you start to speak about someone (as I spoke about Peter) and get excited or upset about that person, that is a projection. Open the door and keep going.

Let me remind you that your projection of the Dreammaker can be a very important dreamdoor. He, She, or "It" may appear in many different forms during the day.

You might suddenly find yourself speaking of great people: of teachers or gurus, of spiritual experiences, or about seeking special moments during the day that give you peace, creativity, and wellness. Sometimes the Dreammaker can be found projected onto sleep and relaxation itself. Sleep may be a form of the Dreammaker because it can give you an incredible and magical view through Its access to other worlds. Your projection of the Dreamer is a supreme dreamdoor. If you find that door, go through it!

Incomplete sentences. When you say, "Well, yesterday you know, I . . . I went down the street and I met so and so, and then . . . [breath], you know [breath], you know . . ."—that is an incomplete sentence, a dreamdoor.

Go through that dreamdoor using secret dreamwork. For example, you might ask the "dreamer": "While walking down the street, did you have a weird feeling? Were others looking at you?" Go through that dreamdoor situation into Dreamland. Who was looking, what did they think? What happened next? Open the door with the person and walk through that into another world.

Foreign words. Occasional foreign words used in otherwise monolingual sentences are dreamdoors.

For example, an American client of mine suffering from depression normally uses English as his main language. He had been depressed for a long time. One day he said to me that he loved eating out in Portland, especially at a certain restaurant where he always ordered a bottle of *Beaujolais*. Now, though *Beaujolais* is the name of a real French wine, the effort he used to pronounce *Beaujolais* correctly made me think this was a dream-door.

I decided to open the door and go into "its" country. So I said, exploring the terrain, "You know, Americans have a lot of fun in Paris." He immediately blushed and said he loved being on the French Mediterranean, especially the Côte d'Azur. I repeated, in sloppy French, what he had just said. "Vous aimez la Cote-du-jour?" In a very suspicious manner, as if he had been caught at something, he asked, "Why are you so interested in the French?" So I reacted to the moment and told him that I was checking up on him.

He got red in the face and, to make a long story short, told me for the first time about a short relationship that he'd had while in France. I insisted that the relationship was so secret that even he dared not think about it. I suggested that he sense that relationship right now. When he tried to do that, he realized that, in fact, he was not as depressed as he had thought. In fact, he was enjoying a hidden sense of happiness right now!

Then he reversed himself when he realized what he had said and explained that he could not be happy; after all, he was depressed! Finally he stood for the truth. In the background, he was having a secret affair with happiness. He was so happy, he cried and admitted that he was just shy about showing it.

175

All that came from *Beaujolais*. Remember that language is rich with Dreaming. Just step through the door.

Repeated or missing words. Words that are missing, repeated, or stressed are dreamdoors. Listen closely, and you can climb aboard and dream.

For example, one of my older clients thought it was time for her to die. She was afraid of the future, and could not imagine that life had anything left for her to do. She told me she was afraid to die, but really, what else could she do? I did not know what to say.

She had no dreams to report, so I decided to listen for the dreaming in her narrative. While we spoke about the future, she kept forgetting a certain word. She said, "In the past, when I was in my hometown, I used to . . . what do you call it, that particular way of helping people?"

I did not know what she was talking about but said, "Oh yes, that thing you did with people, it was very special."

"You know," she said, "I loved doing volunteer work at the hospitals. It was so fulfilling."

"Volunteer work at the hospitals" was a Dreaming trying to arise. She thought she should be preparing for her death because the future had nothing in store for her. Now she got interested in helping others and went to work at a hospice. All this happened more than twenty years ago, and today my client is still alive and helping others.

Exaggerations. Exaggerating, or not being completely truthful, is a dreamdoor.

In the beginning of *Journey to Ixtlan,* the shaman Don Juan is telling his apprentice Carlos Castaneda that lying was not the problem for a warrior. It was the beginning of the "nagual," a journey into the unknown. Apparently, Castaneda lied when he first met the shaman, bragging that he, Castaneda, was a great healer. Don Juan later explained that Castaneda did not take responsibility. Don Juan did not care if his apprentice was honest, but he did care that Castaneda take responsibility for "his lie," for being a great healer. He needed to unfold that lie!

Exaggerations are dreamdoors: Practice unfolding them, believing them, doing them, realizing them.

Dreamdoor Examples

To demonstrate the exercise that concludes this chapter, I shall briefly describe my work with a few people. This work may give you a few more hints and the encouragement you need to try all this for yourself.

Arny: Hi, June, how did yesterday go for you? Tell me about your-self and how you experienced yesterday.

June: I didn't feel well yesterday when I woke up. So I went back to sleep and slept half the day. [An exaggeration!]

Arny: No kidding. You slept *half the day?* That means you slept all night and then another twelve hours.

June: Not quite, but yes, sleeping felt great.

Arny: Sleeping, sleeping. What happened while you were sleeping?

June: I started feeling better. I told myself before I went to sleep that I would wake up when I felt better.

Arny: [Sleeping for another twelve hours is a bit of an exaggeration, a dreamdoor.] How amazing. Hmm. . . . This reminds me of a story about a woman who was kind of sick, so she went to a healer who put her into a full trance. The healer said, "Go deeply inside, go back to the world of sleep, and go to sleep for many days. When you are in the land of sleep, without even trying, magical things will happen and you will be well when you awaken. Don't work at anything, leave it all in my hands. Learn to relax and not work so hard." The woman shivered and went to sleep. Healing events occurred while the woman was deeply unconscious. The healer was indeed a very special woman. . . .

June: [Now joining in] Yes, the healer did not even have a body. She was beyond the body. Larger than a body, she was a goddess [very shyly] who watched over the sick woman [cries].

Arny: And when the woman awoke, she knew God was very close. . . .

June: Yes, that is what was missing. And after that, she promised herself not to get so far from God again!

In this example the exaggeration of sleeping half a day was used as a dreamdoor to open up to what turned out to be nurturing her relationship with God.

Let me give you one more example of using dreamdoors.

Harry: A couple of days ago, I was on a plane, a 747, and watched a movie. There was a kid in the film; the kid was taking off in an airplane, pulling the airplane out of the hangar.

Arny: [The child is a third party, another dreamdoor!] That was such a child! Really an unusual little kid.

Harry: All this reminded me of my own childhood, and how much I wanted to fly.

Arny: [Thinking of the past, childhood, as another dreamdoor, I stressed the child in Harry's film.] And that child was amazing!

Harry: Yeah, in the film the kid flew for the first time. He was a courageous kid. He fastened locks to the pedals that worked the rudder so he could reach the controls. He was barely able to reach the pedals.

Arny: Didn't he look down suddenly and get afraid?

Harry: No, the kid didn't get frightened, but everyone else was!

Arny: You mean that kid wasn't afraid to risk his life for something? My god, he risked his life? That is an amazing child! He risked his life to play, experiment, and do what he wanted to do. Doing the impossible was his goal. Following his dreams.

At this point, Harry began to laugh excitedly. Shyly, then with more courage, he began to tell about his own life and how he is longing to take incredible risks he has not had the courage to take before.

In this example, the child is a third party who was not-here, not-now, and a dreamdoor through which Harry found courage.

Sounds and Music

Before doing the final exercise, I want to briefly discuss how tunes can be dreamdoors. Some people hear sounds in a very special way, or mistake one sound for another sound. Everyone has had the experience of tunes suddenly popping up in our minds.

Figure 30. Tunes can be dreamdoors.

Spontaneously arising songs or tunes can be incredible dream-doors revealing the Dreaming of the moment. In the exercise that will soon follow, I will talk about a "first" and a "second" song that come to mind, because the order in which tunes come to mind is apparently the order of steps from the conscious mind deeper into the Dreaming.[30]

For example, if I ask myself right now what tune comes to mind, the first song I think of is the "Volga Boatman," a song that describes working people moving slowly down a river, working on a boat. On the other hand, the second song that comes to mind is much different, much livelier—it is the Howdy Doody song—and it's about a puppet, inviting kids to play. The words are: "It's Howdy Doody time, it's Howdy Doody time, it's Howdy Doody time, so kids let's go!" While the first song describes where we are with our conscious minds at a given moment, the second song leads us directly into the Dreaming.

While my everyday mind is like the men working on the boat moving down a great Volga River, the song about the puppet gives me the feeling of the Dreaming, of being a child, playing in an imaginative world. If I were to open the dreamdoor and follow the second song even further, I would enter an imaginative sce-nario, change worlds, and identities, and thoroughly enjoy myself.

Instead of going further with my process just now, however, I want to suggest to the reader to explore his or her own dream-doors; songs, foreign words, exaggerations, and so on.

In the following exercise, which can be done alone or with another person, I suggest that you talk (or gossip) with yourself, or chat with the other person. To make things easier, talk about what

---

[30]The process-oriented therapist, Lane Arye, discusses the use of music in detail in his fascinating *Unintentional Music* (Hampton Roads, 2001).

happened yesterday. You will have to listen closely for words and tunes, the dreamdoors to pass through into the Dreaming. Listen carefully to yourself or the other.

The "Reality As a Dream" Experiment

As I have said, you can do this experiment with yourself or with another dreamer. In either case, whether you're working alone or with another, you shall be noticing dreamdoors and valuing them. You may need courage to go through some of them and then dream on into the story that emerges from them.

I suggest, if possible, that you place your notebook nearby. (An audiotape or videotape recorder could be useful—but not necessary— to record your moment-by-moment process so that you can hear the dreamdoors when playing back the narrative.) Remember to consider the possibility that everyday life is not "real," in the way we typically use this word, but a dream not unlike the nature of our nighttime dreams.

If you are doing this exercise with someone else, you may, at one point or another, forget that you are Dreaming. Who you are and who the other person is may, for short moments, become blurred. Don't worry about that. The Dreaming entangles the two of you. Let blurring happen; it is part of the enchantment of it all.

For the benefit of all, you can bring yourself back into everyday reality at the end of the exercise by asking questions about everyday reality and relating experiences to the here and now of the dreamer. Enchantment is important, but in the overall democratic view of altered states of consciousness, sober consensual awareness is just as valuable.

Secret Dreaming with Dreamdoors

Make a note about a dream you recently had. If you or the person you are working with has not had a dream, all the better. After all, everyday life is a dream. However, if you or the other has had a dream, make a note of that now; you can use it later to check the work you will soon do. The dream was about . . .

Ask yourself or your partner what has been happening in everyday reality, and notice feelings, moods, and problems that are searching for solutions. Write down what happened yesterday. What important events happened? If nothing outer happened, what inner events occurred? What moods or feelings did you notice?

1. Dreamdoors. Look, listen, and notice dreamdoors. Notice the use of the past and the future tenses. Make a note about this now. (Remember, the past is happening now in the Dreaming.) Check on sentences that were difficult to complete. Notice projections onto people or objects. Remember that you can explore the world of your projections by gossiping into them. Notice complexes and emotionally charged topics. (Remember that you can open these dreamdoors with a curious and innocent attitude exploring everything you hear.) Were there missing words? What were they? Note repeated words (repeat them some more!) Also note foreign words (remember to enter their country!) Were there exaggerations?

Remember, you can take those exaggerations as a tale, as a dream wanting greater and more congruent expression. What body symptoms have you or the dreamer been thinking about? What uncontrolled movement experiences have you noticed, if any?

Now choose from the above what you suspect are two or three of the most powerful dreamdoors:

1. _____

2. _____

3. _____

Go through those dreamdoors and notice how co-creation happens. Enter the atmosphere of one of those dreamdoors and, feeling into that atmosphere, begin to create a story using the dreamer's problems, Dreammaker figures, and other dreamdoors. Gossip, exaggerate, and explore the world of the future and past.

2. Now imagine that you are hearing music. What's the name of the first song you hear just now? Name it or note some of its words. How does it go?

Now think of a second song, a second tune and its words, if you can remember them or if there are any. What are the words, if any, of the second song? Hum that second song to yourself. Hum that piece of music again now.

Hearing, feeling, and humming the music, continue to tell your dreamdoor story. Remember to include the three most powerful dreamdoors—whether they be the dreamdoors of complexes, incomplete tales, exaggerations, or mistaken, repeated, or missed words. Go into them and through them.

If you need more help with secret dreaming, filling in the blanks (. . .) in the following tale might be helpful.

Once upon a time, there was a woman [or man] with this uncanny and unsolved problem (. . .). Around her were various figures, both known and unknown, such as (. . .). She came from a particular economic scene, social situation, and racial and ethnic situation (. . .). Her body went through the most unusual states; for example (. . .). Her mind circled round and round certain themes of (. . .), and about certain people, such as (. . .). Not able to solve her problems, she went on as she did every day, trying to do her work in life, which was (. . .).

Finally, when she had decided there was nothing more that she could do, she heard an awesome tune come out of nowhere.

[Hum the second tune that came to mind, feel it, sing it, let its atmosphere prevail.] This tune changed the world around her. She felt differently about everything. At this point a voice spoke and a vision appeared to her in the form of a wise figure who sang, in the rhythm and atmosphere of the music (. . .).

She could hardly believe her ears or eyes and begged for greater clarity. It spoke again, this time for the last time, saying, in that special tone of voice, "My dear child, (. . .)." This time she got the message. This time she heard the Dreammaker's second song and message and was determined to put it into practice in her everyday life. She promised herself to remember the message (. . .), especially when she was doing (. . .) and being (. . .).

Still, a question lingered in her mind. She was troubled and called out into the emptiness, "Where, when, how can I deal with those aspects of life that hinder me from living the way you suggest?" Silence reigned as if forever. Nothing moved.

Then, in its gracious and beneficent manner, the Dreammaker-Songmaker appeared again. This time, It entered right in her body, exactly where she used to have symptoms at one time or another, namely, in her (. . .). In that very area she could feel Its wisdom resonating within her body. From that area, she could hear that music's message [hum again that second song] (. . .). It said, in a healing voice, "My dear, (. . .)." This time she breathed deeply, and her breath helped her get the message; even her body received what it needed, and she knew how to live in everyday life.

3. When you and the dreamer are ready, retell and sing the story. Enjoy it, and dream it on. What is its point? Remember and value your everyday life. Consider the moods that you have been having and how everyday life could change if you kept your new story in mind.

If you recorded a dream in the first step of this exercise, compare your story to that dream. What does your story teach you about your dream? The story tells you that your dream means (. . .). Is there something missing in the dream that you can find in the story? Yes, (. . .) is missing. Is there anything missing in the story that you find in the dream? (. . .)

Allow your dreamwork to be musical and creative. Dreamwork is about learning to change levels of consciousness and gaining access to the Dreammaker's creativity.

Politics and Dreamwork

A politician I once worked with had persistent paranoid fantasies that someone in his audiences might kill him. One day, while I was working with him, he thought he heard someone playing music on the radio of an automobile outside of my office. He heard what he called "gangster music," and as usual, was very afraid, thinking that music came from someone who would kill him. Since he said he never dreamed, I decided to use music as a dreamdoor, and to go deeper with him.

I asked the politician to think of another tune, a second song, not necessarily one coming from outside my office. After a few minutes he said he heard "Amazing Grace," music he used to sing in church. He shyly sang the following words.

> Amazing Grace, how sweet the sound
> That saved a wretch like me.
> I once was lost, but now I'm found.
> Was blind but now I see. . . .

I repeated for him, "I once was lost, but now I'm found, Was blind but now I see." He explained that this song touched him, though he could not explain why. Before he could change the subject, I launched into a little story and told him that there must have once been a man who feared he would be killed by an attacker. One day, this man went to church hoping God would help, because nothing else could. I said that this man must have heard the song, "Amazing Grace," sung by a preacher who had learned to believe in God. The preacher sang the following words, "Amazing Grace, how sweet the sound, That saved a wretch like me."

At this point, my client could no longer contain himself and wept when he heard the "preacher's words." My client explained, "Grace is just the thing I never believed in, it could never happen to me. And now it has." He said he was relieved at least for the time being, from those dreadful paranoid fantasies.

I told him the story and sang "Amazing Grace" again, and our session was completed. Years later, grace did happen to him, in wonderful inner and outer ways neither of us expected at that time.

 ## Things to Remember

1. Dreaming is always knocking on your door in the form of music, body symptoms, complexes, fantasies, fears, special words, the future, and the past.

2. To live a creative life close to Dreaming, go through those dream-doors and use spontaneous music to discover unexpected revelations.

12

Cosmic Principles

In this final chapter, I will compare the new dreamwork we have been studying to the physics of the universe. In the earlier chapters of this book, we have been focusing on training awareness to follow the Dreammaker's clues while working with dreams. We have discovered that we can know about other realms such as dreamdoors, dreams, flirts, and the Dreaming by the way in which these worlds impinge on our perception.

Now let's consider the cosmos as an analogy to our dreamwork. Let us say that the events in the cosmos that appear to us on Earth are analogous to perceptions we receive from the Dreaming. In a way, dreams themselves are like meteorites; that is, falling pieces of stars that strike the Earth, creating craters and carrying messages from the universe beyond. We know about the outer universe, in part, because of the lasting impressions or craters those meteorite stones make on the Earth. Likewise, we know about the Dreaming from dreams that make lasting impressions upon us, which we remember during the day.

Figure 31. Dreams are like meteorites.

However, not all meteors hit the Earth, but instead fly by the atmosphere of the Earth with lightning speeds, skimming the outskirts of this world, flaming brightly because of friction with the Earth's atmosphere. These meteors are like flirts. You have to be a "fast cat" to catch them because they do not hit the Earth, nor do they leave a lasting impression as meteorites do.

Flirtlike meteors help us understand why some people think they do not dream. Most meteors never hit the Earth! However, since all meteorites were once meteors—that is, since all dreams were once flirts—we can still sense the messages from the universe, that is, from the great Dreaming, by working with flirts!

Now let us ask: What happens during days in which neither meteors nor meteorites—that is, neither dreams nor flirts—appear to us? That is a very hard day to imagine, and in fact, it may even be theoretically impossible. Nevertheless, let's pretend such a day really does occur, or at least we marginalize and ignore the flirts and dreams we have had. In this case, there may seem to be no dreams or flirts to reveal the message of the Great Spirit. Well, then, how do we know what the Dreaming is trying to tell us?

Using the cosmos once again as an analogy, even if we did not look up into the sky to see the stars and meteors, we would still know that some force is out there because water in large basins like lakes and oceans periodically moves up and down, making waves. Variations in the gravitational pull of the moon make water waves. Waves remind us of the forces of the universe, even when we do not see meteors or meteorites.

Analogously, the Dreaming makes waves in everyday life in the form of dreamdoors. Dreamdoors are waves—periodic, everyday problems that rise and fall, problems we call issues, complexes, and other people. If we did not know about gravity, we might think the "little you" causes the waves, and if we did not know about the Dreaming, we might think that the little you causes what we call "problems" and dreamdoors in everyday life.

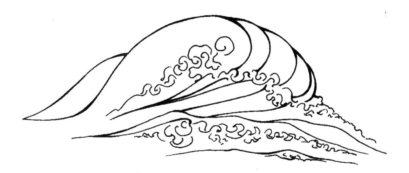

Figure 32. The Dreaming makes waves in everyday life.

Like gravity, the Dreaming is nonlocal in principle. It is everywhere. Therefore, most "problems" or waves must be nonlocal as well. I know of this nonlocal source of problems because of the waves of e-mail I receive. Many people write me about their problems. I can tell that there is a periodic coming and going of problems that determines the increases and decreases in my e-mail! My problems are not just caused by me; there must be a nonlocal element behind those dreamdoors.

The point is that the Dreaming, like the universe, has many ways of expressing Itself. It appears as flirts or meteors that fly by the outer atmosphere as shooting stars; as dreams or meteorites that hit the ground making craters we remember; and as waves in life or gravity making waves in the ocean. Though we cannot see the Dreaming or gravity, we feel their effects.

The newer dreamwork paradigm, centered on the Dreaming, expands older paradigms that focus on the little you and the significance dreams have for your everyday life. In the older paradigms, understanding and following dreams are central tasks. In the newer paradigm, experiencing the Dreaming is central. In the newer one, training the dreamer's awareness of altered states of consciousness is central: *knowing and understanding occur almost spontaneously from these awareness experiences.*

The newer paradigm includes valuing dreams, but also encourages us to open up to Dreaming and perceive Its manifestations as momentary relationship gestures, body problems, breathing experiences, and presignals or flirts. The newer Dreaming paradigm is based on experiencing preverbal, sentient phenomena and on Its images in Dreamland and everyday reality. Dreams themselves now become only one of the important Dreammaker's manifestations. Dreams are not as central as they used to be.

Looking back at my own development, it seems as if the Dreaming paradigm made me place more emphasis on the magic of the moment and less upon dreams. Perhaps that is why I put aside the study of dreams for many years. For a long time, they were my first love in Jungian psychology, my original fascination. I still worship dreams, but now I realize that they are but one of many possible, equally valuable expressions of that awesome altered state of consciousness behind what physicists describe as quantum waves, and meditators experience as the "void."

Your Future in Dreaming

Your interest in dreams affects them, just as they affect the way in which the conscious mind changes. Over time, working with dreams and noticing the Dreaming changes you. If you are in the mood of a so-called average person who is not overtly interested in dreams, you tend to remember them only when they are strong enough—when meteorites leave a big enough crater on the Earth. The "average person" is a passive onlooker who examines dreams only when they are so dramatic they cannot be overlooked.

A more curious onlooker studies her dream, the crater, so to speak, and what it means for her everyday life. An even more fascinated dreamer begins to wonder where her mysterious dreams come from. She traces the crater to the meteor, and the meteor to the universe beyond, so to speak. She learns about dreams, flirts, and Dreaming.

As her relationship to the meteorites expands to an interest in the whole cosmos, she experiences the whole universe as alive and pulsating, with a mind of Its own. She no longer focuses on the crater or meteorites, but on the amazing, creative presence that surrounds her day and night, and her role in this universe.

As her relationship with the Dreaming increases, we can no longer properly speak of an observer and a meteorite, a dreamer and a dream, but rather of the two merging into the Dreammaker and Its apprentice, the Dreammaker and Its mirror. This brings her closer to the sense of creation. She no longer thinks only about the images of her dreams; more often, she feels the impulses behind the images, stories, and other perceptions. It is as if she went through the dreamdoors, then the dream, and then the flirt, to experience the secrets of the universe.

This reminds me of the ecstatic dreamlike visions that occurred to C. G. Jung during his near-death experience, his first heart attack in 1944.[31] He tells us in his autobiography, *Memories, Dreams, Reflections,* that during that near-death experience, he found himself one thousand miles above the Earth. From that viewpoint, he had a grand overview of much of the planet. He noticed near him in space an enormous rock, "a tremendous dark block of stone, like a meteorite. It was about the size of my house, or even bigger. It was floating in space, and I myself was floating in space."[32]

He goes on to say that this stone reminded him of "temples" he had seen on Earth. He knew that if he went into that temple, he would discover the truth about who he really was, where he had come from, and what would come after him. However, before he made this discovery in his dream, he was recalled back to Earth. He survived his heart attack, went back into life, and later died in 1961.

Jung's temple, his "meteorite," may not be all that different from the "meteorites," that is, the flirts we have been studying. Flirts are a kind of temple, a place where we can discover some of the secrets of life, death, and the universe. Moving back and forth, into and out of those flirts, into nonlocality and back into time and space, is part of the new dreamwork paradigm. By getting into those meteors, you can learn about the origins of dreams, perhaps the origin and nature of the universe.

Jung realized that his life was a channel for the Dreammaker. He wanted to know his own and Its nature. Like Jung, Albert Einstein

---

[31]He reports on these remarkable visions in chapter 10 of his autobiography, *Memories, Dreams, Reflections.*

[32]See *Memories, Dreams, Reflections*, page 290 and the following pages.

also wanted "to know God's thoughts, the rest is details."[33] Today we can say that the invisible and ineffable source of the universe may not only be hovering at the outskirts of reality, one thousand miles from the Earth. We need not wait for another incarnation, distant in time, or a near-death experience to know where we come from. In fact, the uncanny source of reality may be right in front of us, in the details of everyday life. The gossip about yesterday, the smells of today, your own unintentional movements and troublesome friends—*these* mundane events are "God's thoughts" or the Dreammaker's temple.

Therefore, the Dreammaker's apprentice realizes her Teacher's temple is the next magical moment in time. Its teachings are like meteorites, meteors, and waves; that is, flirts, irrational events, and dreamdoors.

---

[33]The full quote from Einstein can be found on the first page of chapter 1 of this book.

Readings

Arye, Lane. 2001. *Unintentional Music: Freeing the Creativity Inside You.* Charlottesville, VA: Hampton Roads Publishing.

Berry, Patricia. 1974. An approach to the dream. *Spring* (Zurich), 58–79.

————. 1978. Defense and teleos in dreams. In *Dragonflies: Studies in Imaginal Psychology*, Irvine, TX: University of Dallas.

Bosnak, Robbie. 1997. *Tracks in the Wilderness of Dreaming: Exploring Interior Landscape through Practical Dreamwork.* New York: Delta Books.

Bulkeley, Kelly. 1996. *Among All These Dreamers.* Albany, NY: State University of New York Press.

Castaneda, Carlos. 1972. *Journey to Ixtlan: The Lessons of Don Juan.* New York: Simon and Schuster.

Coxhead, David, and Hiller, Susan. 1975. *Dream Visions of the Night.* London: Thames and Hudson.

Delaney, Gayle. 1996. *Living Dreams.* San Francisco: HarperSanFrancisco.

Freud, Sigmund. 1953. *The Interpretation of Dreams*. New York: Basic Books, (originally published in 1900).

Garfield, Patricia. 1997. *The Dream Messenger: How Dreams of the Departed Bring Healing Gifts*. New York: Simon and Schuster.

—. 1991. *The Healing Power of Dreams*. New York: Simon and Schuster.

Gendlin, Eugene. 1986. *Let Your Body Interpret Your Dreams*. La Salle, IL: Chiron/Open Court.

—. 1962. *Experiencing and the Creation of Meaning*. New York: Free Press.

Hall, Calvin. 1966. *The Meaning of Dreams*. New York: McGraw-Hill.

Hall, James. 1991. *Patterns of Dreaming*. Boston: Shambhala.

Hillman, James. 1979. *The Dream and the Underworld*. New York: Harper & Row.

Houston, Jean. 1982. *The Possible Human*. Los Angeles: Jeremy P. Tarcher.

James, William. 1976. *The Varieties of Religious Experience*. London: Collier Macmillan (originally published in 1902).

Jung, Carl. *Collected Works of C.G. Jung*. Translated by R.F.C. Hull, edited by Gerhard Adler, Michael Fordham, and Herbert Read. Princeton, NJ (Bollingen Series 20): Princeton University Press. (The years of publication vary by volume, as listed below.)

—. Vol. 8. 1969. Structure and dynamics of the psyche. In *On the Nature of Dreams*.

—. Vol. 9, part 1. 1968. Archetypes and the collective unconscious.

—. Vol. 12. 1976. Psychology and alchemy.

—. Vol. 14. 1968. Mysterium coniuntionis.

—. 1961. *Memories, Dreams, Reflections*. New York: Random House.

Kaplan-Williams, Stephen. 1990. *The Elements of Dreamwork*. Dorset: Element Books.

Koch-Sheras, Phyllis R.E., and Hollier, Ann. 1983. *Dream On: A Dream Interpretation and Exploration Guide for Women*. Englewood Cliffs, NJ: Prentice Hall.

Koch-Sheras, Phyllis R.E., and Sheras, Peter. 1991. *Dreams and the Couple: Natural Partners*. Paper presented at the Association for Sleep and Dreams Conference, Charlottesville, VA.

Krippner, Stanley, and Dillard, Joseph. 1988. *Dreamworking: How to Use Your Dreams for Creative Problem Solving*. New York: Bearly Limited.

LaBerge, Stephen. 1991. *Exploring the World of Lucid Dreaming*. New York: Ballantine Books (reprint).

Mansfield, Victor. 1995. *Synchronicity, Science, and Soul-making: Understanding Jungian Synchronicity through Physics, Buddhism, and Philosophy*. La Salle, IN: Open Court.

Mbiti, John. 1997. *African Religions and Philosophy*. Oxford, England: Heinemann Publishers.

Miller, Robbie. 1998. *The Two Hands of God: The Marginalization of Psi Phenomena*. Master's thesis. Portland, OR: Process Work Center of Portland.

Mindell, Amy. 2000. *Metaskills: The Spiritual Art of Therapy*. Portland, OR: Lao Tse Press.[34]

———. 1999. *Coma: A Guide for Friends and Helpers*. Portland, OR: Lao Tse Press.

Mindell, Arnold. 2000. *Dreaming While Awake: Techniques for 24-Hour Lucid Dreaming*. Charlottesville, VA: Hampton Roads Publishing.

———. 2000. *Quantum Mind: The Edge Between Psychology and Physics*. Portland, OR: Lao Tse Press.

———. 1996. *The Shaman's Body: A New Shamanism for Health, Relationships, and Community*. San Francisco: HarperCollins.

[34]Lao Tse Press, P.O. Box 40206, Portland, OR 97240-0206 USA. Telephone: 503-222-3395.

————. 1988. *City Shadows: Psychological Interventions in Psychiatry.* New York, London: Penguin.

————. 1987. *The Dreambody in Relationships.* New York, London: Penguin.

————. 1985. *River's Way: The Process Science of the Dreambody.* London, Boston: Penguin.

————. 1998. *Dreambody: The Body's Role in Revealing the Self.* Portland, OR: Lao Tse Press (originally published by Sigo Press, Boston, 1982).

Morris, Jill. 1985. *The Dream Workbook.* Boston: Little, Brown and Company.

Moss, Robert. 1996. *Conscious Dreaming.* New York: Crown Trade Paperback.

Perls, Fritz. 1969. *Gestalt Therapy Verbatim.* Moab, Utah: Real People Press.

Tart, Charles. 1969. *Altered States of Consciousness.* New York: John Wiley & Sons.

Ullman, Montague, and Zimmerman, Nan. 1979. *Working with Dreams.* London: Hutchinson and Co.

Von Franz, Marie Louise. 1974. *Number and Time: Reflections Leading Toward a Unification of Depth Psychology and Physics.* Evanston, IL: Northwestern University Press.

Index

Hampton Roads Publishing Company

... for the evolving human spirit

Hampton Roads Publishing Company
publishes books on a variety of subjects,
including metaphysics, health, integrative medicine,
visionary fiction, and other related topics.

For a copy of our latest catalog, call toll-free
(800) 766-8009, or send your name and address to:

Hampton Roads Publishing Company, Inc.
1125 Stoney Ridge Road
Charlottesville, VA 22902

e-mail: hrpc@hrpub.com
www.hrpub.com

Dream Doors (167)
172

Archetypes
151 patterns (Jung)